While every precaution has been taken in the preparation of this book, the publisher assumes no responsibility for errors or omissions, or for damages resulting from the use of the information contained herein.

THE DISAPPEARANCE OF LAUREEN ANN RAHN

First edition. July 14, 2021.

Copyright © 2021 Ruth Canton.

ISBN: 979-8215512814

Written by Ruth Canton.

THE DISAPPEARANCE OF LAUREEN ANN RAHN

RUTH CANTON

Laureen Ann Rahn

Early Life

Laureen Ann Rahn was born on April 3, 1966 in Manchester, New Hampshire, to Judith Rahn. The identity of her father has never been released, and it is unclear whether Laureen had any clue as to who he was. Laureen and her mother lived in an apartment complex on Merrimack Street. The two of them were particularly close, always making sure that they spent a lot of time doing things together. Whenever Judith had a date, she would always bring Laureen along. For the most part, Judith was always dedicated to raising her daughter the best way she could. Laureen was smart, a dedicated student, and rarely got into any trouble. She always made good grades, and Judith never had to worry about her daughter's schooling. Laureen enjoyed dancing and singing, and had big dreams of becoming an actress one day.

She went on to Parkside Junior High, and she kept up her grades. However, she started experiencing teenage angst, and would start acting out time and time again. She got into trouble a couple of times, but it was never anything serious. At around this time, she may have started indulging in a little alcohol with friends. She never got extremely drunk, and Judith did not seem to know about her daughter's social experiments. At some point in time, Laureen began telling her school friends that she was about to change schools. She claimed that she was shifting residences, and that they were moving to Florida. After a while, Laureen was no longer attending Parkside, although they hadn't moved out of Manchester. A year later, a few of her Parkside friends discovered that she had shifted to Southside Junior High, and that she was still living with her mother on Merrimack Street.

Disappearance

By April 1980, Judith was dating a man who played tennis, and they would often attend matches out of town. Laureen was always a part of the Saturday outings, and the three would often come back home late into the night. Laureen would always look forward to those outings, and was just as excited as her mother to accompany her mother's boyfriend. On April 26, 1980, Judith was planning another out of town tennis trip with her boyfriend, and as usual, asked Laureen whether she wanted to tag along. In response, Laureen stated that since spring break was just starting, she preferred to just stay home alone. She stated that she wanted to have a quiet day alone, and she asked her mother to go on without her. Judith asked Laureen to ensure that she kept the doors locked, and not to let anyone in. She kissed her daughter goodbye, and told her that she loved her. Judith then left for the trip.

Laureen seemingly had plans for the day, and they did not involve staying home alone until her mother came back. At some point in the evening, Laureen called two of her friends to come over to the house. It was a male friend and a female friend. Once in the house, the trio started drinking. There were a few beers and a bottle of wine, and they spent the time telling stories and joking around. At some point in the night, the male friend heard voices in the hallway, and assumed that Judith had come back earlier than expected. Not wanting to get in trouble for drinking with underage girls, he asked Laureen to let him out through the back door. He claimed that he heard Laureen lock the door behind him. After leaving the apartment, he went home.

Judith finally made it back home sometime after 1 a.m. on Sunday morning. The first thing that she noticed was that all the hallways were uncharacteristically dark. As she made her way to her third floor apartment, the normally well-lit hallways and stairs were completely plunged in darkness. She did not think much about it, and assumed that there must have been an electrical fault, or that a fuse had blown. When she got to her door, she found it closed, but unlocked. This made her a bit angry, considering she had told Laureen to ensure that she kept the doors locked. More bizarre still, the back door was not only unlocked, it was also slightly ajar. She locked both doors and went to check on her daughter. At this point, there seems to be different accounts of what transpired that night.

In the first account, Judith went to check on Laureen, and saw a figure huddled under the blankets. Assuming that it was Laureen, she went to sleep. Later in the morning hours, she woke up and went to check on her daughter. This time around, she realized that it wasn't Laureen in the bed. Laureen's female friend was the one asleep in the bed. When asked where Laureen was, she stated that Laureen had taken a pillow and blanket to go sleep on the couch. Judith saw the pillow and blanket, and quickly realized that Laureen was missing. Remembering the unlocked front door and the open back door, she grew concerned and called the police.

In the second account, Judith locked the doors and then went to check on Laureen. She saw the figure under the blankets and assumed that her daughter was asleep. She then started her nighttime routine, preparing for bed. This took a little while. Once she was ready for bed, she went back to Laureen's bedroom, hoping to talk to her about the unlocked doors. When she turned on the light, she realized that it wasn't Laureen in the bed. She woke the friend up and asked her where Laureen was. She explained that Laureen was asleep on the couch. Judith noticed that her daughter's purse and personal belongings were still in plain view, and she got worried. She immediately called police. The call was made at 3:45 a.m.

Initial Investigation

When the responding officers showed up at the apartment complex, they took note of the darkened hallways. When they got to Judith's third floor apartment, they spoke to Laureen's friend, asking her to account for the night's activities. She mentioned that they had been drinking, although she did not reveal who actually provided the alcohol. The house was neat, and there was no sign of a struggle. Apart from Judith finding the doors unlocked and open, she stated that nothing seemed out of the ordinary. The house was almost exactly as she had left it, and nothing was missing except Laureen. Judith maintained that her daughter would not have left willingly, despite how it may have seemed to officers. However, the police immediately assumed that Laureen had run away.

Despite their assumptions, officers proceeded to canvass the neighborhood, searching for any clues as to where Laureen might have headed to. They tracked down the male friend that was present at the house. He maintained that he left soon after he heard the noises in the hallway, and that Laureen did lock the back door behind him. When asked whether he may have heard wrong, he denied it. He stated that he clearly heard the lock click into place. Police soon cleared him as a suspect.

Officers made a bizarre discovery during their canvassing. They found that there had been no power problem that caused the hallway lights to go out. The reason was much more sinister. All the bulbs had been unscrewed, just enough to kill the lights. This was the case for every bulb, from the ground floor to the last floor. This made some of the officers assigned to the case to start entertaining the idea that Laureen may have been abducted. Two camps quickly emerged, one with officers who believed that Laureen was a runaway, and another with officers who thought she had been kidnapped. As the days passed by without any word from Laureen, more officers began to believe in the possibility that there had been foul play. Laureen did not carry any of her clothing, including her purse, her brand new sneakers were still on the living room floor next to the couch, and the hallway light bulbs.

Officers began circulating Laureen's missing person flyer, and news outlets in the area picked up the story. At the time of her disappearance, Laureen was last seen dressed in a blue plaid blouse, a white V-neck sweater, brown shoes, a silver-blue necklace, and a heart-shaped gold ring. She had brown hair and blue eyes, 5'4, and 90 pounds. Her face was plastered on the front page of the local newspapers, and by this time, officers had more or less unanimously agreed that she had been abducted. The police department assigned more uniformed officers to the case to help follow up on the tips and leads that were being called into the station. Unfortunately, the leads almost always led to a dead end. All officers could uncover were rumors that there was a fourth person at the house that night, a man. However, the other two friends maintained that there were only three people in the house that night. As the days went by, the tips trickled down, and the officers were assigned to other cases. Laureen's case quickly became a cold one.

California Connection

Six months after Laureen's disappearance, Judith was going through her phone bill when she noticed three charges that she did not recognize. All the calls were made in July, three months after Laureen had disappeared. Judith reached out to investigators about the charges, hoping that it would be useful in finding her daughter. There were three unrecognizable charges, with phone numbers Judith insisted she had never dialed before. When police traced the numbers, they found out that the calls had originated from California. One number belonged to a motel in Santa Monica, another to a motel in Santa Ana, and the third one belonged to a teen sexual assistance hotline. When police followed up on the calls made from the motels, they came up empty. They turned their attention to the hotline number, which was linked to a doctor in California. When asked about the calls, the doctor maintained that he knew nothing about it. When he was shown Laureen's picture, he stated that he had never seen or met her, and had no idea who she was. Police were bummed. They cleared the doctor as a suspect, and the case went cold again.

However, Judith maintained that the calls were made by Laureen. She had no relatives or friends in California, and she could not think of anyone else who could have made the calls. Additionally, Laureen had been looking forward to becoming an actress and Hollywood star, so it seemed plausible that she might have ended up there. While Judith was convinced that Laureen made these calls, police weren't so sure. There were two ways that anyone could have charged the calls to Judith's number. The caller could have called the phone company and requested for a special PIN number. If the person satisfactorily proved that they were the owner of the account, the company would give them the PIN. This could have been used to make calls from virtually anywhere, and Judith would be charged. Alternatively, dialing zero, then Judith's number, then the recipient's number was enough to make the call on Judith's bill. This second method is what investigators believed was used. It bypassed the need to call the phone company and prove ownership.

Silent Calls and 1981 Sighting

Surprisingly, the phone charges weren't the only oddities in this case. A few months after Laureen disappeared, Judith began receiving silent calls. The phone would ring, and the person on the other end would remain quiet until Judith hanged up. The calls were infrequent when they started, but began getting increasingly frequent when the holiday season drew closer. Even more chilling was that the calls came in at 3:45 a.m., the same time Judith had called police on the day Laureen disappeared. When Judith told her sister what was happening, she was shocked to find out that her sister was also receiving the same calls. By the time Christmas Day came around, the calls were coming in almost on a daily basis. Judith finally stopped reporting them to police, and decided to wait until the person on the other end finally spoke up. She ended up finally changing her number in the mid-80s, years after Laureen's disappearance.

Sometime in 1981, Judith received a call from one of her relatives. She stated that she had seen Laureen – or at least, someone who closely resembled Laureen – at a bus stop in Boston, Massachusetts. When asked whether she approached her, the relative said that she didn't. However, she was pretty adamant that it was Laureen she saw. Police followed up, but they were unable to confirm that it was indeed Laureen.

1985

Ever since her daughter disappeared, Judith believed that there was something her friends had kept secret about the events of that fateful night.

Even though she knew that they had been friends for years, she was convinced that they had not been forthcoming with the police. However, their stories remained consistent every time they were questioned by police. In 1985, the male friend that was present in the apartment that night took his own life. When Judith heard of this, she started wondering whether the young man's death had any connection to her daughter's disappearance. Investigators decided to look into this, and they discovered no connection between the suicide and Laureen's disappearance.

Judith, still reeling from the pain of her daughter going missing, decided to seek some answers herself. She hired a private investigator to pick up the case, and check for new leads. The investigator followed the police's course of investigation, up to the three mystery phone charges. Looking to find more answers, traveled to California to check if he could find any information about who may have made the calls from the Santa Ana and Santa Monica motels. Unfortunately, there was no way to find out who had been staying at the motels during the time the calls were made. However, he spoke to officers who had helped in the investigation, and he was told something that had never been mentioned before.

According to the officers, the two motels had been in the police's radar in 1980. They were bases for a number of sex trafficking rings at the time. The investigation into the trafficking rings had uncovered that the leader at the time was known as Dr. Z. They never found out his real name, and the activities had long since been moved out of the motels. The investigator then turned his attention to the teen sexual assistance hotline hoping to uncover more information. Expecting the doctor to maintain the same story he told in 1980, the investigator sought the help of the local police. When they got to the doctor's residence, they found out that he had an entirely different story. This time, he told officers that he did not run the hotline, and that his wife did. He stated that runaway girls would show up at the house looking for his wife, and that Laureen may have been one of them. He stated that he wasn't the one who was in contact with the girls, but he did remember seeing Laureen at the house sometime after she went missing. He could not offer any further details. However, he remembered that Laureen was at one point with Annie Sprinkle. He told the officers to look for Sprinkle if they needed more information, and that Sprinkle may have a clue as to where Laureen was.

The officers were familiar with Sprinkle's name, and this steered the case into an unexpected direction. Annie Sprinkle was a pornographic actress, and had been featured in a number of movies by 1985. They figured that if Sprinkle's knew Laureen, then it was likely that the 14 year old had been abducted by sex traffickers. When investigators finally tracked down Sprinkle, they were once again disappointed by the information they received. Sprinkle claimed that she had never met Laureen, and that her friendship was with the doctor's wife. She admitted that she knew about the hotline, but that she never personally got involved with any of the girls. When asked whether Laureen may have been at any of the motels, she claimed that it was impossible. At the time, the motels were also used as sets to shoot the porn films. The sheer number of people who walked through those sets was enormous, and Sprinkle maintained that she never crossed paths with Laureen. The doctor's credibility was higher than that of Sprinkle, so investigators decided to dig a little deeper to ensure that Sprinkle was at least truthful. Officers collected Sprinkle's films, dating back to 1980, after Laureen disappeared. They watched the videos closely, checking to see if Laureen was present in any of the scenes. She was not. With no information tying Sprinkle to Laureen other than the doctor's word, investigators cleared Sprinkle. The case was back to square one.

1986 Phone Call

By 1986, Judith had changed her phone number. The silent calls had stopped after the change, and her sister followed suit. At one time during the year, Judith received a call from one of Laureen's childhood friends. Roger Maurais told Judith that he was out of the house when a call came in, and his mother picked up the call. She told him that on the other end of the line was a woman asking to speak to Roger. She stated that her name was either Laurie or Laureen. Roger's mother didn't catch exactly what name was given. The caller claimed that she had been Roger's girlfriend a few years back. When she told the woman that Roger wasn't home, the caller hung up. Because Laureen had been missing for six years, Roger had deemed it important to inform Judith just in case it would help in finding her. This information gave Judith hope. She started believing that Laureen was still alive and that she had tried to reach out. The assumption was that Laureen had dialed all the numbers she remembered, but found her mother and aunt unreachable, so she opted to talk to an old friend. Unfortunately, investigators were unable to pinpoint where the call originated from. Judith was crushed.

1988 Sighting

In 1988, eight years after Laureen disappeared, a man called police and stated that he may have seen her. The man stated that he lived in Anchorage, Alaska, and that he had seen a prostitute standing on one of the streets. According to him, the prostitute matched Laureen's description, and he was sure it was her. Investigators asked the Anchorage police to follow up on the man's claims. They went and interviewed him in a bid to check whether he was credible or not. After they determined that the man was telling the truth, they went to the street to search for the prostitute. Unfortunately, they were unable to find anyone matching Laureen's description. They stated that a lot of time had passed, and she may have moved to a different street.

Other Disappearances

As the years passed by with no new clues as to what could have happened to Laureen, investigators began combing through other cases. They were hoping to find other disappearances that share similarities with Laureen's case. The first was that of Rachel Elizabeth Garden. Rachel was a 15 year old who disappeared on March 22, 1980, just a few weeks before Laureen's disappearance. Garden was last at Rowe's Corner Market in Newton, New Hampshire. She had purchased gum and pack of cigarettes, then started walking along Main Street towards her friend's place where she was supposed to spend the night. She never arrived, and she was reported missing at 10 a.m. the next morning. Police theorized that she had run away, but her family was adamant that Garden would not leave her belongings, or her beloved horse unattended. A witness came forward and stated that he had seen Garden speaking to three men in a car. They had criminal pasts, but police couldn't find any evidence that tied them to Garden's disappearance. One of the men eventually confessed to killing Garden, and even gave police the location of the body. Investigators searched the area, but no evidence was ever recovered.

The second case was that of Shirley Ann McBride. 15-year-old Shirley was last seen on July 13, 1984, at around 9:30 p.m. She had left her sister's apartment in Concord, New Hampshire, and was planning to pick up some money she was owed, and then head over to her boyfriend's workplace in Concord Litho. She was never seen again, although it took several days for her family to report her missing. Shirley had a habit of going away for several days without calling or telling anyone. However, this time all her belongings were still in her sister's house, and her boyfriend hadn't seen her either. Police categorized her as a runaway, even though her family insisted that this was not the case. A few days later, police began suspecting foul play, and they questioned the boyfriend. He was cleared as a suspect, and there were no further leads. Shirley's family declared her legally dead in 1996, 12 years after she went missing.

The third case was that of Denise Ann Daneault. Denise was a 25-year-old divorced mother of two who lived just two blocks from Laureen's apartment complex. She was last seen on Sunday June, 8, 1960, just two months after Laureen went missing. At the time, she was living with a roommate on Hayward Street in Manchester, New Hampshire. She had attended a private social club that night, and was last seen leaving, the downtown Manchester club at around 1:30 a.m. She told people that she was heading to another party, and was never seen or heard from again. Despite their age difference, Shirley closely resembled Laureen, and investigators started wondering whether their disappearances were connected. When they started looking into Shirley's case, they found out that she was living a few doors from a man named Bob Evans. Evans was actually Terry Peder Rasmussen, who later became a suspected serial killer. Police began wondering whether Shirley and Laureen were victims of Rasmussen, who was suspected of killing four women and putting their bodies in drums, and then dumping them near Bear Brook State Park in Allenstown, New Hampshire. Several searches were conducted in the search for Shirley, with one even taking place 37 years after her disappearance. Her body has never been recovered.

Investigators combed through the four cases looking for any clues whether they had a serial abductor in the town. The four women all disappeared within a thirty-mile radius of each other, under eerily similar circumstances. However, nothing concrete ever arose from this line of investigation. All four cases remain open.

Aftermath of Laureen's Disappearance

The private investigator hired by Judith wasn't able to uncover more information, and Judith finally had to stop the investigation. She believes that Laureen is still alive, and wonders how her daughter's life has been since she disappeared in 1980. When asked about the three phone charges, Judith maintains that it was Laureen who had made them, and efforts to convince her otherwise have been futile. Referring to the night of the disappearance, Judith is adamant that Laureen's childhood friends knew more than they told police, and that they were either afraid of something or someone.

In the mid-1980s, Judith got married and relocated with her husband to Florida. A few years later, she began consulting psychics. None of the psychics she consulted ever expressed seeing Laureen in the afterlife, and this solidified Judith's belief that Laureen was still alive. Despite her daughter having been missing for almost 40 years, Judith still hold on to hope that she is alive and well somewhere in the world. However, authorities are not so optimistic, and they strongly believe that Laureen was a victim of foul play.

BRITTANY HOLBERG

Brittany Holberg was a twenty-three years old prostitute when she was convicted of murdering 80-year-old A.B. Towery Jr, stabbing him over sixty times.

The controversy surrounding the case centered around the relationship of Brittany and Towery prior to the killing. Brittany argued that Towery was a client who went into a rage when he found drugs on her person. He attacked her and she retaliated in self-defense.

Further investigation would reveal otherwise, however, as Brittany would use numerous household items in a brutal assault on the elderly man.

She fled the scene only to be caught at a McDonald's after police received a tip from a witness who saw her on "America's Most Wanted."

With her good looks and well-proportioned body, Brittany has remained in the spotlight as she was featured in a Maxim Magazine article as one of the "hottest women on death row".

Brittany still sits on death row today with her case being appealed on the numerous levels in the court system.

EARLY LIFE

Brittany was born on January 1, 1973, in Amarillo, Texas.

Accounts on Brittany's home life vary as she would manipulate according to the needs of her listener. To her probation officer, she informed them that her home life was "good" and that she "had everything that she ever wanted". She would often describe her mother as her best friend.

During other occasions, however, Brittany would paint a different story.

She would describe her parents as being "hippie-drugsters". Brittany would state that she was close to her mother but never knew her father, a heroin addict who was in and out of the Texas prison system. Her mother would later marry a man named John Schwartz with the couple marrying and divorcing four times.

They would drink heavily and openly smoke weed in front of the young Brittany who would be sexually assaulted by a babysitter at the age of five. When she was twelve, one of her aunts was murdered and according to Brittany "everything fell apart" at home. Her parents would leave her unattended as they indulged in pot and booze.

"They just stopped working," Brittany said. "They just let everything go."

She would be gang raped by two men who confronted her in an alley behind her home when she was thirteen.

Brittany would then spend the majority of her time living with her grandmother. By the age of sixteen, however, she would run away with her boyfriend Ward. The two would make it as far as California, get married, and have a young daughter named Mackenzie.

The union would not last long, however. Brittany would divorce Ward and move back to her native Amarillo. Ward would take Mackenzie and move to Tulsa, Oklahoma.

Brittany would state that she suffered a knee injury and would become addicted to pain medication during treatment. She would then graduate to harder drugs like cocaine.

In and out of rehab, Brittany's life spiraled out of control. She could manipulate with the best of them, however, and would escape from the Midland Halfway House with the help of a female counselor.

Brittany would hang out with the drug-using crowd and her own habits were out of control. To support her addiction, Brittany began working as a prostitute.

This would put her in harm's way on many an occasion as she would get gang-raped and beaten severely.

The assault would put her in the hospital but she would resume "tricking" when she was released.

"At that point in her life, Brittany was incorrigible," forensic psychologist Paula Orange said."Numerous people had reached to her and tried to help. She had extended family members trying to help. Friends trying to help. Even church outreach workers. All to no avail. The drugs had taken root and she was dead set on manipulating everyone around her. Family, roommates, church members, doctors, dentists, and pharmacists would all fall victim to her schemes to get drugs."

By 1993, Brittany was a full-blown drug-addicted prostitute with the rap sheet to prove it. In April of that year, she would steal a gun from her step-father. She then passed over $1300 in "hot" checks and applied for several store credit cards using a fake name.

Brittany and one of her aunts would run a scam on dentists, lying to them about their pain levels in order to get prescription medication. When the prescription drugs ran out, she would return to street drugs like cocaine and heroin. Arrests would follow and Brittany would be charged in Hale County with drug possession, paraphernalia, and public intoxication.

Upon her release, Brittany would proceed to steal her mother's car and forge checks in her name. The prostitution continued unabated as well as she stole the wallet from one of her "tricks" who pressed charges.

While in jail for the theft, Brittany would be introduced to Ella Gibbs and Patricia Karnes who ran the ministry in the Randall County Jail. The women tried to get Brittany on the right track and introduce her to Christianity.

"I wanted to reassure Brittany that she is a valuable person, that her life has great potential, and that this is the mortal portion of an eternal life," Karnes said. " Brittany is an eternal being and through the many prayers from my [prayer] group [in Lubbock,] I have been led to come back into this child's life to support her here, to encourage her, to find her courage from the Holy Spirit within her, and to let her know that there is a human being mortal person who will stand beside her and see the good in her and support whatever God plans for the rest of your [sic] life."

A.B. TOWERY

Towery was by all accounts a nice man. His son would bristle at the idea that he was Brittany's "sugar daddy".

"Dad wasn't a dirty old man," his son said. "Dad was just trying to help somebody and look what he got, and now she's getting three meals a day and a warm place to sleep."

The defense would later bring up the fact that he once pulled a knife on his son Russell during a temper tantrum. Towery would have a history with prostitutes (according to court testimony). Connie Baker would be a prostitute from the 1980s to 1997 and stated that Towery was one of her clients. Baker would also claim Tower as a client but she also had a history of drug possession and auto theft. Diana Wheeler would also admit to being one of Towery's prostitutes in the years of 1994 and 1995. She had come to his home and he even went so far as to clean the stains off his Mel Mac dinnerware. But Wheeler also had a long criminal history like Baker, arrested for prostitution, criminal trespass and giving false identification to a police officer.

The controversy at the trial was if Brittany and Towery had an ongoing "sex-for-money" relationship.

This would be vigorously discounted by family members.

His daughter-in-law would come to the home and help with some housekeeping. His sons would also visit daily and never report any "ladies of the evening" coming to visit their father.

The picture just didn't fit.

Brittany stated she was sent to Towery's place by a fellow streetwalker who went by the moniker of "Green Eyes" but that it was later revealed that no such prostitute by that name existed. Brittany had lied like she had so many times before.

The two seemed to have met by chance.

COMING BACK FROM THE GROCERY STORE

November 13th, 1996 was another normal day for the 80-year old A.B Towery. He had just purchased groceries at an Albertson's store and was walking back to his apartment. As he entered the courtyard, he was approached by the 23-year old Brittany Holberg.

She asked to use his telephone and Towery consented. He wanted to help the sweet-voiced Brittany and didn't believe that she posed any kind of physical threat to him.

What he didn't know was that Brittany was coming down from a cocaine high and had not slept in ten days.

"Brittany could be persuasive," Orange said. "She was well-versed in how to charm people, she knew exactly what to say and do in terms of body language. She was like a trained actress. It didn't take much cajoling on her part to convince Towery to let her inside his home. He probably thought 'what's the big deal?'"

Once inside, Brittany would demand money from the elderly man but he refused. Brittany then attacked Towery, trying to strong arm the wallet out of his pocket. The struggle began in the living room. The two then pushed and pulled each other around a partition that separated the kitchen from the living room. They then returned to the living room. At some point, Towery tried to leave the apartment but Brittany pulled him back in. The evidence also indicated that the two paused during this 45-minute fight, catching their breath and nursing their wounds. Brittany would sustain minor stab wounds to her stomach and thigh.

"This was most likely a fight that had a lot of clutching and grabbing," Orange said. "There was less blood in the living room so the conjecture is that is where the fight started. There was blood near the door so that suggests that Towery was bleeding out and trying to escape for help. Remember, he was a slow-moving 80-year old man. Brittany was a young woman but she was fueled by cocaine. He's getting tired a lot faster than she will."

Eventually, Brittany gained the upper hand. She used various objects around the home to beat down Towery. She started with a cast iron frying pan, then a steam iron, a claw hammer, a fruit knife, a butcher knife and then two forks. Towery would fall to the floor, a bloody mess.

Brittany then took a lamp and shoved its base five inches down his throat which choked him to death.

Satisfied that he had finally killed Tower, Brittany removed her bloody clothes. She washed up in his bathroom then went to his closet to find some clothes that fit her.

Walking back to his dead body, Brittany retrieved the wallet out of Towery's pocket. She took out the $1400 dollars he had and dropped the now empty wallet onto his stomach.

Brittany casually walked out of the apartment and hitched a ride with a young couple. The couple dropped her off at a local crack house where Brittany paid them off with two $100 bills (which had blood stains on them). Inside the drug den, Brittany befriended the proprietor and changed clothes again. She then went to a local hotel with hundreds of dollars worth of cocaine and indulged.

TRIAL

Brittany's defense attorney, Catherine Brown Dodson, would argue that Holberg acted in self-defense when she killed Towery. Her primary argument was that Towery was far from an innocent, elderly man. He was, in fact, a drug abuser himself who became physically violent with Brittany when he found a crack pipe on her person. He then hit Brittany two times in the head when she turned her back to him. Brittany retaliated and ultimately put the lamp post in his mouth in an attempt to end the fight.

Brittany then fled as she believed that no one would believe her side of the story because she was both a prostitute and a drug addict.

While in jail, Brittany would try to coerce Katina Dixon, her cellmate to kill Vickie Marie Kirkpatrick who was the prosecution witness.

Towery's history with prostitutes would be brought up in court testimony. They would also mention incidents of violence with his ex-wife and children but jurors didn't believe the old man was in any type of shape to employ the service of a prostitute.

"My father didn't even like the word 'sex'", one of his sons said. "He was old-fashioned."

A psychiatrist would testify, however, that Brittany had battered wife syndrome, post-traumatic stress disorder, and cocaine addiction.

The jury did not take long to deliberate, finding Brittany to be a cunning, manipulative liar who committed one of the most brutal crimes in the history of Amarillo.

They would find her guilty and Brittany would be moved to death row at Gatesville, Texas.

"I can't even explain to you," Brittany said in a magazine interview. "What it's like to have someone say 'You are sentenced to die.' It's words. You feel helpless, numb. It's almost as if your emotions shut you down."

Brittany would spend her first few weeks in prison laying prone on her bed in a zombie-like state. Over time, she grew accepting of her situation. She knew she was going to die but made it a point to learn to take each day one step at a time.

Her inspiration for cleaning up her act came from the memory of her daughter Mackenzie.

"I cannot live," Brittany said. "And I cannot die, knowing that my child has to live with the horror that these people tried to say about me, the story of the crime, their depiction that I was a cold-blooded person."

Brittany states that she dedicates her days to reading, writing to family and working on her law appeals. She also is anti-death penalty advocate.

She would follow other Texas inmates who were now on death row and make appeals on their behalf, specifically that of Betty Lou Beets.

"I realized," Brittany said. "It doesn't matter whether I'm guilty or innocent, this has now become a very political thing... At this point, they're just killing to kill."

She complained that after a recent jail uprising, the treatment of death row inmates has worsened.

"You would not believe the treatment we are given," Brittany said. "Just two weeks ago, we were informed that not only would we be strip-searched for our one hour of recreation a day, but also when taken for a shower. So for the last two weeks, we have been stripped no less than six times a day. This is every day, sometimes at times like 2:30-3 a.m., and we never leave the building or our cells for that matter."

As of this writing, Brittany's stay of execution has been appealed and appealed for the past eighteen years.

Her attorneys would exhaust the appeal process in the state system but it is now in the federal courts.

Her case, however, has been costing taxpayers "conservatively to be at least $400,000" according to county criminal attorney James Farren. In the future, he has decided to forgo seeking the death penalty in capital cases.

Farren continues to favor a death penalty but only under certain circumstances like "a guy walks into a day care center and kills the children or if someone kills a police officer or a firefighter in the line of duty."

Farren predicted that Brittany would remain on death row for another five years at least. "They can go through the U.S District Court in Amarillo, then it can go to the Fifth U.S Circuit Court and the U.S. Supreme Court. Then from there it can go back to the U.S. District."

But the appeals can come to a halt if the district judge refuses to hear it again.

"If the Supreme Court says 'no,'" Farren said. "That's when the district judge can feel safe in stopping this process."

The entire process has been an infuriating one for the Towery family. His son both rages and mourns about what happened to his father.

"She tried to apologize to us during the trial," Russel Towery said. " I got up and walked out. I'm sure other families are going through the same things I'm going through. It's been almost 19 years ... people forget."

"I don't want to die before she does. I want to stand there as she's kicking and screaming going to the death gurney. I want her to think about what my dad went through when she didn't even know his name," he said. "She thinks that because she said she was sorry, that everything's all right. ... she is evil and needs to be destroyed."

NO WAY OUT : THE TRUE STORY OF AMBER CUMMINGS

20

SARAH CAMDEN

On the surface, James and Amber Cummings had it all.

They had been married for twelve years. James had inherited millions of dollars from his father and they owned a home in the peaceful, seaside town of Belfast, Maine.

"On paper, they were a couple that looked as if they had everything," forensic psychologist Paula Orange said. "Definitely one of those cases where looks are more than deceiving. They are downright deadly."

The couple met in Fort Bragg, California. Amber was a tall brunette while James was overweight and had an awkward vibe about him.

Amber found him charming, however, and would later describe him as the "nicest guy she'd ever met." She would marry him at 19 years of age and things looked bright for the young couple until Amber got pregnant.

"That is when his personality started to change," Orange said. "He would drive away Amber's family members in California and seek to keep her isolated. This brought much consternation to Amber's side of the family, obviously. There was one heart-breaking instance where Amber's mother and sister went to a neighbor's yard just to get a glimpse of Amber's daughter riding her tricycle."

James wanted no outside influence on Amber or their daughter so he began moving the family around. They left California when Amber turned five and moved to Texas. Then they traveled the country in a motor home until 2007 when the finally settled in Belfast, Maine.

"My husband said that he hated people and that he didn't care where we moved," Amber said. "I always wanted to live in a nice, small town in Maine."

EARLY LIFE

James' life seemed to have been one of trouble even though he was born into wealth.

His father would be murdered by one of his former employees in 1997 which was preceded by James making headline news as he videotaped his own mother doing heroin.

James would have numerous run-ins with the law himself.

"He had a bunch of assault charges," Orange said. "Some were cases where he was the victim. Others were cases where he was the perpetrator. When he was the perp, his father's money always bailed him out."

According to some Internet rumors, James' father had allegedly injured himself while getting off a forklift on one of the docks in the Fort Bragg harbor, breaking his knee in the fall.

Cummings then went to a friend's house and fell to the ground outside claiming that he "tripped in a hole." James' father then sued the owners of the property and won.

"That gives you an idea of the kind of guy James' father was," Orange said. "Rumors abound on the internet and in the Fort Bragg community about how he acquired his wealth. None of it is verifiable aside from the fact that the majority of the trust is funneled through a trailer park, which is odd."

Cummings Sr. would own many businesses and it would be one of his employees, a man named Williams Vargas who would gun him down.

Vargas detonated a homemade bomb he called a "firecracker" outside Cummings' home. The disgruntled employee then panicked as one of Cummings' neighbors drove by and blocked his escape. Cummings Sr. then came out with his own gun to investigate the blast which shattered his window.

Vargas then pulled out his own gun and shot Cummings. He had been working for Cummings at the Noyo Harbor trailer park and was allowed to live there in exchange for labor. But he began having problems with other residents which he would blame Cummings Sr. for.

Cummings, 77 years old at the time of his murder, had built his wealth by running restaurants, motels, a fish-processing plant as well as trailer parks. He also owned the Depot Mall shopping center and a McDonald's restaurant.

``Jim was quite an entrepreneur. He had quite a lot of land holdings, in some key areas, really, in the harbor and other areas around,'' former City Manager Gary Milliman said.

James Jr. would be the beneficiary of his father's death. He would tell people that he made his living "selling off Texas real estate" but the truth was that he was a trust fund kid living off the businesses that his father created.

The trust fund started off by giving Jams a whopping ten million dollars a year. The funds would deplete rapidly, however, as James would have a six-year legal battle against trustees whom he thought were mismanaging the money.

His mental illness would grow worse as his finances decreased.

NEO-NAZI SYMPATHIES

"He would go on daily rants about Barack Obama," Orange said. "Which would seem harmless at first until Amber realized that James was, in fact, a white supremacist. He began spending his days hunting down rare Nazi artifacts on the Internet and purchasing them."

James had applied to the National Socialist Movement, one of the largest neo-Nazi clubs in the country. He had written numerous white supremacy organizations on-line and began to mix toxic chemicals in their kitchen sink while telling Amber about his desire to make a "dirty bomb."

James had hired a pair of contractors to paint the interior of the house. The painters would later testify to witnessing James berate his wife. He would tell the men about his guns and go on about Adolf Hitler.

Thinking he had an eager audience, James bragged about his collection of silverware and plate settings that he claimed to have been used by Hitler himself.

"Check this out," James showed a swastika flag to the painter. "This was real. Not a knock-off. They actually waved this same flag while Hitler spoke."

James would run his household as if he were Hitler himself, marching around the home wearing a black hat and uniform with a Nazi armband.

Working himself up into a Nazi-like frenzy of rage, he would then abuse Amber physically, emotionally and sexually.

"He stripped away whatever self-esteem she had," Orange said. "He had no friends himself and didn't allow her to have any either."

As the years went by, James developed paranoid schizophrenic tendencies which had given birth to ideas that grew more bizarre with time. The married couple slept in separate bedrooms and James had guns placed under both of their pillows "just in case."

On one occasion, Amber left the home for an extended period of time. James immediately became enraged upon her arrival back. He demanded to know where she was and who she was with. Amber had gone to meet with a home-schooling group which they both previously agreed would be a good idea.

James went ballistic, berating Amber and throwing his sharpened Nazi knives against the wall.

CHILD ABUSE

James did not limit his abuse to Amber. His paranoid anger soon extended to their daughter, Clara.

This became evident to Amber when their daughter had come across James' collection of Nazi knives and began examining them.

"Leave those alone!" James screamed as he ran into the room and grabbed the box of knives away from the girl. "These belonged to the Führer! The Führer!"

Amber had very little self-esteem left, but she intervened when James would physically abuse their daughter. She would throw herself between the two and take the beating herself.

This would only incite James further as the would beat Amber then march up to Clara's room and continue his abuse.

"He kept them isolated and feeling helpless," Orange said. "They tried to escape on a few occasions but he caught them, keeping them locked in the house. She thought he had some kind of superhuman power."

CHILD PORNOGRAPHY

Seeking new outlets, James' mind became so perverted that he soon began indulging in child pornography. He showed his collection to Amber who shuddered in horror.

"Which one do you like best?" he would ask his wife, pointing to a series of pictures on the scream.

In addition to the child pornography, James began teaching his daughter to see the world through his racist viewpoint.

"This is equal-opportunity hatred," he preached to his daughter. "We can hate everybody."

"He was deluded," Orange said. "He actually saw himself as the second coming of Hitler. He began seeing his daughter as his future helper, someone who would be in charge of 'reconditioning' women and children after he declared war on the United States."

James wanted to build a torture chamber in the basement of the house. He told Amber about his desire to kill people and "peel the skin off their bones." He also obsessed on the Showtime television series, "Dexter", which featured a serial killer as the protagonist. James would then take long walks around the Belfast area, daydreaming about living out his 'Dexter' fantasy.

"He constantly talked about the different ways of killing and torturing people and hiding their bodies," Amber said. "He used to say it was a need in him."

THE FINAL STRAW

"The abuse happened incrementally for her," Orange said. "It is easy to sit back and judge a person like her, saying that she should have just left. But she was like a frog in a pot of cool water before it starts to boil. The abuse started small at first then bit by bit it increased as her self-esteem diminished. But when it came to protecting her daughter, she had to act."

One December 9th, 2008, Amber Cummings finally had enough.

She got up like she normally did after another night of abuse by her husband.

"Amber discovered James messing around with the chemicals in the kitchen," Orange said. "He said that he would bury her in the backyard if he said anything."

She sent her daughter downstairs to eat breakfast while she pulled out a .45 caliber pistol from underneath her pillow.

Then she held the gun underneath her own throat.

"Amber's first thought was to kill herself," Orange said. "But then she saw her daughter's doll in the room. She shuddered to think of her daughter spending the rest of her childhood with her father as she realized that it was only a matter of time before James' obsession with child pornography would make him do something to Clara. So she had to seek an alternative course of action."

Amber would later tell court-appointed psychologists that James' infatuation with child pornography and his "sexual attraction to young girls" made her believe that he was becoming obsessed with their daughter.

Fueled by her protective maternal instinct, Amber entered the bedroom where James was sleeping. She never had any gumption to stand up for herself when James abused her.

But when it came to protecting her daughter, a whole new Amber showed up.

She pointed the gun at the back of James' head and fired. Blood splattered against the bedpost. Shocked by her own display of violence, Amber sprinted down the steps and ordered her daughter to go to her neighbor's and stay there.

"If it wasn't for my daughter, I would have committed suicide years ago," Amber said. "Some of the mental torture will never leave me the rest of my life. It was so severe, it will be with me every day."

Amber then called the police and told them what she did.

"It's hard for us to justify shooting somebody who's asleep in the bed," Sheriff Jeffrey Trafton said. "But when we arrived she looked more like a victim than a killer."

"She was in a state of shock," Orange said. "She had finally taken action to free herself from years of abuse. The state, of course, cannot let such a deed go unchecked."

A CONSPIRACY AFOOT?

As police investigated the murder scene, they discovered another James Cummings secret.

He was gathering materials to make a "dirty bomb."

Fueled by his white supremacist ideology, James planned to go to Washington, D.C for Barack Obama's presidential inauguration. Once there, he would set off his dirty bomb.

"He had all the ingredients inside the garage," Orange said. "The FBI found the instructions for the dirty bomb. There were four 1-gallon containers with uranium, thorium and beryllium powder. There were numerous other jugs which contained lithium metal, thermite, magnesium ribbon, black iron oxide and other explosive substances. James Cummings meant business and there is clear evidence he was going to follow through on his plan. Whether he could have pulled it off is another story."

Had his plan gone to fruition, James could have potentially killed hundreds of people. Amber saved not only herself but innumerable lives by killing James herself.

"The stuff that he had wasn't dangerous," Bangor Police Chief Jeffrey Trafton said. "In its present form, it wasn't dangerous to the community. Technicians told me what you had to do, you had to get real close for a long period of time before it would have any effect as far as the radioactivity. When the stuff was found, obviously detectives from the state police came and we didn't know what it was. But there was no danger to the community. That was established fairly quickly. But my involvement since it was handed over to the state police has been little to none."

THE TRIAL

Amber would remain in a state of shock after the murder. She worried more about her daughter's well-being than her own. She was fully prepared to go to jail.

"Her mental state was still askew after she killed James," Orange said. "She probably saw prison as a welcome respite from her abusive life. She had been in 'prison' already and saw the jail system as a safe place."

Amber would plead guilty during trial proceedings. Her story would make the media rounds, however, and she soon found numerous supporters in her small Maine town. People showed up wearing "Free Amber" t-shirts.

"There was no way in hell a jury in that vicinity would have found her guilty," Orange said. "None."

Amber seemed to have found leniency on both sides of the judicial system. Her attorney and the prosecutors would come up with a plea deal which called for a sentence of up to eight years but with Amber serving no less than a year. This would be followed by six years of probation.

Her attorney then recommended to the judge that Amber spend no whatsoever behind bars while the Assistant Attorney General, Leane Zania, wanted Cummings to spend a year in jail.

"This kind of 'self-help' is severely anti-social behavior," Zania wrote. "It will be punished accordingly."

During the course of the trial, Amber would not take the stand in her defense. Three mental health experts who had counseled her after the killing all affirmed the fact that Amber had endured traumatic abuse. They advised the judge not to send her to jail.

The psychiatrists had given Amber a diagnosis of "shared psychotic disorder" which in layman's terms meant that she had absorbed some of his craziness just by being around him.

"You don't hang out by the outhouse without getting a rash," Orange said. "So that is how Amber was able to endure all of that psychological trauma. She became so desensitized to it that it became the norm after a few years."

The judge sentenced her to eight years in prison but it was a suspended sentence, allowing her to go free.

"The terrible thing is, I was forced to take the life of someone that I loved very much to save my daughter that I love very much," Amber said. "It's something that I will have to live with for the rest of my life, and it won't be easy. I'll always wonder. I'll always be looking over my shoulder, always wondering if he can come back from the dead."

In her public remarks, Amber requested that the community forgive her husband and not have any anger toward him.

"I just want to thank the community and people of Maine," Amber said after leaving the courtroom. "Because without them, I don't think my daughter and I could have made all this progress. Really, really wonderful caring people. If I was anywhere else, we wouldn't be doing this well. I believe that with all my heart."

"The people around here are pretty incredible. They gave me the benefit of the doubt, and a chance to prove myself. There was a lot of support, an unbelievable amount of support, in Belfast. People came out and took care of us and made sure we had everything we need."

Amber stated that after she shot James that she fell into a "state of shock and numbness." She would continue to dream about James, having nightmares about him choking her.

Since then, she dedicated herself to trying to undo the mental damage James did to her daughter.

"I hope to raise a really good kid, who cares a lot about people," Amber said. I hope she ends up strong and can take care of herself. I think she will."

BONUS STORY: DEATH ROW GRANNY

It never ends.

No way.

No way am I letting this man demean and degrade me another day.

He's just like my father.

A binge drinker. And the binges were happening more and more.

He's on the road to nowhere and taking me with him.

It never ends.

First my father. Now him.

Fuck it.

I threw the cigarette on the blanket. I knew it was flammable.

Then I watched the smoke rise and smiled.

In Lumberton, North Carolina, Thomas Burke fell victim to a house fire which was caused by a burning cigarette. Investigative authorities thought that he had fallen asleep while smoking, leaving thirty-eight-year-old Velma Burke as his widow.

They didn't know that the fire was set by Velma.

Velma knew how to play the part of the grieving widow. She cried and gave the authorities the requisite crocodile tears. No one would believe that the murder of Thomas Burke would set off a series of killings performed by the seemingly kind and harmless church-going woman with the soft voice.

EARLY LIFE

Velma Bullard grew up as the second of nine children in the rural part of Sampson County, North Carolina.

Times were tough for the Bullard family. They would live on a small farm with no electricity, running water or an outhouse.

"They had to go outdoors," forensic psychologist Paula Orange said. "The entire family had to endure the indignity of going into the woods or using pots to shit and piss."

The home was small and cramped for the nine children. Velma would be forced to sleep in the same bedroom with her parents until the age of five.

Her father was a loom repairman (fixing an apparatus that was used to weave clothing) and an abusive alcoholic. Velma had an older brother, Olive, who were subject to his nightly beatings. Lillie, her mother, was too meek to protect her children from her husband's violent outbursts.

"She had the type of father who would not need any provocation," Orange said. "He would take out the pettiest frustrations, like not being able to find something around the house, and take it out on the children. Velma would become resentful toward her mother who was too weak or indifferent to stop her father from beating on the kids. She accepted his discipline as 'the way it was.'"

Velma would find school as a welcome escape from her dreadful home life. She loved her teacher and was an excellent student during her early grade school years. When she would return home from school, she took solace in the fact that her father would always arrive home late as he worked long hours at the textile mill.

"Her father Murphy had that Protestant work ethic in him," Orange said. "He accepted the long hours and low pay, seeing a kind of nobility in that. Only problem was, he would binge drink. Not store bought alcohol but homemade moonshine. After a couple of shots, he would be 'lit' and inflict his wrath on everyone in the house."

By the age of eleven, Velma would be forced to take on various chores around the farm. She would clean up the house, washing and iron everyone's clothing (eleven people). Her father would chastise her for not mending or sewing his work clothes properly as well.

"Her father was a stern taskmaster," Orange said. "Hell, you can say 'slave driver.' He would have Velma come home early from school days when the laundry got too backed up. Velma hated this and felt embarrassed. Her family didn't have much and as she grew older her classmates began to see her for what she was, a poor girl that was an easy mark for teasing."

Velma would grow to be 5'3" but gain weight as she got older. She would be mocked about her obesity, her shoddy clothes the gap between her two front teeth. She would also be called "knot head" after she ran head first into a boy at school which left a permanent contusion on her forehead.

By the age of twelve, Velma seemed to have taken on all of her mother's duties. She would cook all of the family meals in addition to performing cleaning around the farm house. She would miss school for days at a time as her father forced her to complete chores around the home before she could continue her education.

"Academic achievement was not at the forefront of her father's mind," Orange said. "Her mother was of little use because of her depression and mental illness. Velma was the oldest girl so she took on the duties of mom at an age where she should have been playing with dolls."

ANGER, ABUSE, AND CHURCH

Despite her father's verbal abuse and alcohol-fueled beatings, the family kept up a face of religious interest. Velma would be sent to Bible school every year until the age of thirteen. During her last year of Bible school, her father marked the occasion by buying Velma a silk pink dress with ribbons. Velma recalled the day as one of the happiest of her life.

The happiness would be short-lived.

Velma would claim that her father raped her when she was thirteen years old. She revealed this only to her pastor in her later years before she stood trial. Velma did not even tell her mother whom she did not think would believe the molestation took place.

"Things that went on inside our home when I grew up," Velma said. "Were kept inside."

At the age of fifteen, Velma continued to excel in school. Despite her chubby physique, she becomes adept at basketball and is pegged to be the team's star player for the upcoming season. But her father did not allow her to play.

"Who is going to iron these damn clothes?" he snarled.

The family then moved to Robeson county and switched from the Presbyterian denomination to Baptist. It was here that Velma would meet Thomas Burke and the two made it clear that they wanted to date. Once again, Velma's father would intervene, telling Velma that she had to wait until her sixteenth birthday until she could date.

The two waited patiently for her birthday to arrive and the following year Thomas would propose to her while they went to the movies.

Knowing that her father would not approve, Velma and Thomas eloped, moving to Dillon, South Carolina. Neither Thomas or Velma had any money as they both quit high school to get married. Thomas then went to work at a local textile mill.

"At this point, I believe that Velma began to realize that her life would not be that much better with Thomas," Orange said. "He literally has the same job as her father."

Economics forced Velma and Thomas to move in with his parents. This arrangement would last for a year until Thomas got a better paying job at a soft drink company.

At the age of nineteen, Velma would give birth to her first son, Ronnie. The couple would then move back to Parkton, North Carolina where they would remain in the same home for eleven years. Two years later, the young couple would welcome a daughter named Kim.

A CYCLE OF RELIGION AND ABUSE

The Burkes would be fixtures at the local Baptist church with Velma taking the reigns to teach a Sunday school class. But the prayers and sermons would do little to offset the growing ennui in the Burke home. Two years after giving birth to Kim, Velma would get hit by a drunk driver while crossing the street. She would be hospitalized for an extended period, suffering both physically and mentally.

Thomas' job at the soft drink company would not be enough to provide for the family. Velma would be forced to leave her small children at home and work in a textile mill just like her father. The couple would have different work hours, with Velma working nights and Thomas working days as they would take turns watching the children.

Velma would fall victim to the hard work at the mill and the stress of raising two young children. She began bleeding and her doctor performed a hysterectomy.

Velma's mother would take pity on the couple and give them one acre of land near their old farm. Thomas would build a three-bedroom home for the family but Velma was already going down a slippery slope. Her personality changed after the hysterectomy, claiming that she always felt "nervous and afraid."

Things would get worse as Thomas suffered a head injury in a car accident. He then began to drink heavily and begin to beat Velma.

"It was deja vu," Orange said. "Velma had, in essence, married her father."

One night, the couple argued and Thomas punched Velma in an alcohol-fueled tantrum. The police are called to the home and Velma sent

Thomas to the state hospital to get treatment for his drinking. Her husband remains there for three days but when he returns home, his behavior is worse than behavior. He's angry at Velma for sending him to the "drunk tank". His alcoholism worsens and he would go on to lose his job because of absenteeism.

"Velma is thirty-five years old at this time," Orange said. "But she's an old thirty-five with crow's feet under her eyes and a hangdog look. She's had a rough life, not necessarily by her own design, and it has taken its toll."

Velma leaves the textile mill but then finds two different jobs in order to support the family. During the day, she works as a sales clerk in a Belk department store. At night, she goes to work as a machine operator in a cotton mill.

Thomas, meanwhile, would continue to drink.

He rages on a daily basis, on one occasion he pinned son Ronnie up against the wall and threatened him with a knife. Velma would faint during the encounter and be transported to the hospital. She was diagnosed as having a nervous breakdown and lapsed into a serious depression. The medical staff gave her tranquilizers to calm down. Velma believed that it was during this stint in the hospital that she became addicted to the painkillers.

"The drugs were helping," Orange said. "When nothing else did. So she wanted more and more."

Velma's children acknowledged that their mother's mood swings were due to the drugs.

Over the next three years, Velma would go in and out of the hospital for drug overdoses. After each visit, her addiction only grew as did her prescription list.

"She fell through the cracks in her own family," Orange said. "And in the system itself. Her family had their own issues to deal with as Thomas would abuse everyone on a daily basis. Finally, Velma did something she could control. She killed her husband."

On April 21st, 1969, Velma would drop a cigarette on the floor of her home and waited until her husband inhaled enough smoke to die.

His death, however, would do nothing to solve Velma's problems.

Her addictions and anxiety would only get worse.

A HOSPITAL FREQUENT FLYER

Velma would have another nervous breakdown after killing Thomas and lapse into a guilt-ridden depression. But seven months later, a co-worker at the Belk department store would introduce her to fifty-four-year-old Jennings Barfield. Jennings had emphysema and diabetes but Velma would marry him anyway. Unlike her marriage with Thomas which started out well, Velma's marriage with the older Jennings would be troubled from the start. Her drug addiction would escalate and Jennings would express his own regret at marrying her.

"I don't know why I married her," Jennings said. "All she does is pop pills all day."

After less than three years of marriage, Velma decided to part ways with Jennings. She didn't file for divorce, however, she decided to poison him with arsenic. She would later claim that she only meant to "make him sick."

Jennings Barfield was already ill and doctors had no suspicion that Velma was behind the death. Arsenic was a slow burn poison that could kill without detection. The autopsy called for no arsenic test and Velma had gotten away with murder once again.

But Seven months later, Velma would overdose on her prescription meds and become hospitalized. Her family recognized the pattern but could not wean Velma off of the drinks. She would remain hospitalized for three weeks.

Her personality seemed to change after the hospital release. She returned to work at Belk department store but kept being combative and argumentative with customers. Her boss knew of her circumstances and tried to coax her to do better. He took her away from the public contact and into the back stock room where he had her put pricing on the clothing items.

Her boss soon realized that Velma's addiction had gotten out of control. Velma would not be able to function in the back room, leaving tasks uncompleted as she would have her prescription medications delivered to the store.

"It is a hopeless situation," the store manager told Velma's son Ronnie before he fired his mother.

BROKE AND DESTITUTE

With no income, Velma would lose the family home as she no longer paid the mortgage. She would be forced to move back in with her parents and face the two people she blamed everything for.

Her father had grown ill, however, and would die from lung cancer shortly after Velma moved back into the home. She would feel bad about her father's death and admit that she had a love/hate relationship with him.

"I had learned to love him as much as I had hated him," Velma said. "He was so good to my kids. I think he tried to do with my kids like he wished he had done to us. He could not stand to see me correct them. If I would pick them up and spank them, he would ask me, 'Isn't that enough?'"

But after her father's death Velma self-medicated once again. She overdosed and was hospitalized for two weeks. Her family didn't judge, they instead thought she was "cursed."

"Velma needed psychiatric help," Orange said. "So she began medicating herself with deleterious results. She would "doctor shop" for different physicians who would be manipulated into giving her the drugs she wanted. Her addiction eventually grows until she becomes desperate for money in order to fuel the drug habit."

A MURDERER AND A THIEF

Velma began stealing from those closest to her, starting with her mother. Her mother confronted Velma about a missing check and Velma went ballistic.

"She had violent mood swings," Orange said. "The medication had completely changed her personality as she needed the drugs above all else. The people around her were not familiar with how to handle a person who had this kind of mental illness. So this made for a very dangerous cocktail for her and anyone close to her."

Hitting a new low, Velma took out a $1,000 loan under her mother Lillie's name. She put up the family home as collateral and forged her mother's signature on the documents. Velma then blew through the money and a month later took out another loan, once again using her mother's house as collateral. The following month, she emptied the checking account on her now deceased husband, Jennings. Two months later, the loan company began sending Velma overdue notices as she had not been paying off the loan.

"In Velma's mind," Orange said. "She had no other choice but to kill off her own mother."

Velma went to the local pharmacy and looked for bottles that had the warning of "fatal if ingested." She put the poison into a drink for her mother and watched as she drank the fatal elixir.

Her mother then began vomiting and lost control of her bowels. Within a few hours, her mother could not so much as walk and an ambulance was called.

Velma came to visit her in the hospital to finish the job. Armed with a Thermos, she made a special concoction of chicken soup and arsenic.

"Drink it slow," Velma said as she tenderly lifted the cups to the lips of her ailing mother. "Slow."

Her mother would eventually die of "natural causes" as no one suspected Velma of committing murder. Instead, she received sympathy.

"So sorry for your loss," hospital staff said.

"The thing with arsenic is that it shuts down the whole system," Orange said. "So hospital staff just chalked up her mother's weakness to old age. Checking for arsenic poisoning would be the furthest thing from their mind."

Velma showed the necessary emotion and received sympathy from friends and family. She then moved in with her daughter Kim and son-in-law Dennis who lived in a trailer park. She could not evade the authorities for long though as the authorities caught wind of Velma's check forgeries.

Velma reacted as she always did. She would run away and medicate herself.

"Her drug addiction kept pushing her into a corner and she saw no way out," Orange said. "So, this time, she goes to her son Ronnie's house and overdoses again, trying to kill herself. She falls and breaks her collar bone which laid her out in the hospital another three weeks."

But the police find her situation unsympathetic.

"We're sorry, Velma," the deputy informed her at her hospital bed. "But once you have been cleared for release, we will arrest you."

Velma would not have that. She tried to overdose again but this go around the hospital staff pumped out her stomach.

She was sent to court the next day and sentenced to six months in jail for the forgery. She is released after four months for good behavior.

NO REHAB HERE

Her addiction still unchecked, Velma returned to live with Kim and her son-in-law. She rummaged through the belongings of her son-in-law and stole a check, forging his name so she can get more prescription meds. Her daughter Kim now has caught wind of her mother's addiction, pleading with her doctors to stop prescribing her.

"In some ways," Orange said. "The doctors were just as guilty as she was. But back in the day, there was no way to cross-reference this stuff like we do now. Once she had her fill with one doctor she would go to the next and the next."

Velma's addiction prevented her from taking a forty-hour a week job. So she looked for alternative forms of income.

She would find a job taking care of the elderly.

Montgomery and Dolly Edwards would be her first clients.

"She found herself some easy targets," Orange said. "There didn't seem to be any legislative body in place that prevents sociopaths from caretaking the elderly. So Velma doesn't slip through any cracks, she just befriends the elderly couple and begins taking care of them."

Montgomery was blind and unable to walk. He was 93-years old and his 83-year old wife was too feeble to take care of him. They paid $75 a week for Velma to become their live-in caretaker.

All was good, at least in the beginning. But Dolly had a sharp tongue and would criticize Velma daily. Velma would keep a nice exterior unless confronted, saw Dolly has yet another wheel in her cycle of verbal abuse.

"It seemed to be a never-ending loop for her," Orange said. "Being forced to deal with verbally abusive people. Velma had long since snapped and Dollie simply had no idea who she was dealing with."

Velma began to plot out Montgomery and Dollie's demise until she meets their nephew, Stuart Taylor.

Stuart was already married but was blown away when he met the caretaker of his Aunt Dollie.

Velma would play it cool, stealing what she could from the couple in terms of petty cash and household items that had value. They outlived their usefulness to her within a year as Montgomery died of "natural causes". One month later, Dolly also passed away.

And again, no one suspected the sweet and soft-spoken Velma to have had anything to do with their deaths.

MOVING ON

Velma saw being a caretaker as a perfect front for her. She could steal as much money as she could and when the old folks detected something amiss she would simply poison them. After killing the Edwards' couple, she set the word out at church that she as available to be a caregiver. The pastor would refer her to Margie Lee Pittman who was seeking for a caregiver for her elderly parents, John Henry and Record Lee.

"She comes here twice a week," the pastor reassured Pittman. "She's a nice, kindly woman. You can't go wrong."

Pittman's father, John Henry Lee, was eighty years old when he discovered that his new caregiver had forged a $50 check on his account. He then fell violently ill, suffering through a spastic spell of vomiting, diarrhea, and convulsions. The doctors would chalk up his quick death to gastroenteritis but in fact, he had been poisoned with arsenic.

Velma played the caregiver role until his end. She attended his funeral and cried with the family, sending an ornate wreath (with money stolen from the dead man) to the proceedings.

For whatever reason, Velma spared Lee's wife and moved back to Lumberton, North Carolina to live in a trailer park. She began working as an aide in a nursing home and received word from Stuart that he was now a widow. The two began dating and she moved part of her belongings into his home.

"Stuart is a nice guy," Orange said. "He has no idea what kind of woman Velma is. She is so manipulative and cunning that the younger man is putty in her hands. So the relationship starts great as she reels him in with kindness and charm."

The couple are happy cohabitating until Stuart Stuart finds a letter addressed to Velma from the state penitentiary.

Curious, he began reading the correspondence and realized that is from a former cellmate of Velma.

Stuart became enraged. He threatened to "expose" Velma to all of his family and friends. Somehow, someway, however, she was able to calm him down.

He then found out that she had forged over $200 in checks on his account. The two argued but stayed together for the next two months.

"Velma had the Christian facade down pat," Orange said. "She asked Stuart to forgive her and the next thing you know they are going to a Rex Humbard revival. But before they went, she poured arsenic poison in both his beer and tea. She made sure he drank every drop."

Returning home from the revival, Stuart started to vomit on the drive home, the poison kicking in.

Velma had to keep the con going. She had to appear like a concerned girlfriend so she called up Stuart's daughter, Alice, later that night and told her that Stuart had came down with the flu.

Stuart's daughter expressed concern but Velma kept her at bay.

"Don't you worry now, honey. I'll take care of everything."

Stuart died the next day.

Velma would speak at Stuart's funeral and tearfully asked for his wedding band. His family graciously allowed her to have it and gave her $400 to help her cope with the grief.

But Alice knew her father was a picture of health. She vociferously argued for more tests beyond the standard autopsy and sure enough, arsenic had been found in Stuart's tissues.

On March 10th, 1978, the sheriffs arrived at Velma's home to bring her in for questioning. She was interrogated for over three hours, holding her ground. But she knows the evidence will trump her denials and tries to commit suicide after being released. This go around, however, her son Ronnie stopped her.

The sheriffs come to visit Velma again and she has one more surprise up her sleeve.

But Velma has one more surprise up her sleeve.

She would confess. Not only for the murder of Stuart but of six others.

"I set my first husband on fire," Velma confessed without an attorney present. "And I killed the rest of them."

"It was almost as if she wanted to be free of the guilt she had been carrying," Orange said. "Her confession seemed to take a burden off her back."

"The last ten years were like that," Velma said. "A drug nightmare. It was a case of not knowing where you are or what you've done."

The bodies of her victims were later exhumed and all tested positive for arsenic.

FACING THE GRIM REAPER

Velma's case would be prosecuted by Joe Freeman Britt, who was listed in the Guinness Book of World Records as the country's "deadliest prosecutor."

Velma would plead not guilty by reason of insanity but the court denied her plea.

"I needed to keep them sick until I could pay back the money I had stolen from them," Velma said. "I wanted to earn their thanks by nursing them back to health. I needed the money. I was addicted to pain killers. Anti-depressants. Amphetamines."

On November 23rd, 1978, Velma's trial would begin in Elizabethtown, North Carolina where she would be charged with the first-degree murder of her boyfriend, Stuart Taylor. The trial lasted seven days and the jury reached a verdict of guilty, placing her on death row at the age of 47. She was scheduled to be executed on February 3rd, 1979 but received a stay.

Velma would be sentenced to death and the verdict was appealed all the way to the U.S. Supreme court. Her attorney maintained that the jury had never been presented with the full extent of Velma's "addiction and background." Velma remained tight-lipped about that to everyone but her pastor. Her attorney felt thought her horrific background could have been used as part of her defense and the jury would have found her to be more of a sympathetic case.

CHANGING SPOTS?

"She's not the same person who went to prison in 1978," Kim Burke Norton, Velma's daughter said.

While in jail, Velma became a model prisoner.

"The first week I was here was the worst week," Velma recalled. "Everything about it."

Velma no longer had access to her drugs in prison and she began to dry out. With daily visits from two different pastors, Velma began to discuss her anger and repressed issues that fueled her addiction and murders.

Velma would claim that as she was awaiting trial in 1978 she came to a "meeting with Christ" that caused her to "change inwardly."

Velma heard a broadcast by radio evangelist JK Kinkle. "Jesus loves you, prisoners, too," Kinkle said. "He died for you too. No matter what you've done, the Lord will forgive you."

After Velma heard this sermon, she dropped to her knees and cried out to God.

She would then become the "go to" counselor for young inmates in the prison.

The inmates would nickname Velma as "Mama Margie" because of her wisdom and she would in turn think of them as her "adopted children."

The prison guards and counselors would take the most incorrigible prisoners and place them in a cell next to Velma. Velma would invariably counsel the young prisoner and advise them on the correct path.

"They'd come in ready to kill themselves," Sister Mary Teresa Floyd said. "And here she was with a death sentence, mothering and helping them."

"Living in prison is a struggle," Velma said. "Even at its best. And I know that without Him and His strength that has sustained me, I couldn't have made it even this far."

Her stay on death row soon became a part of the news brief. During this time, a phalanx of evangelists would take her cause to the mainstream. The Reverend Hugh Hoyle would become Velma's personal minister as she received stays of execution in September, October and December of 1981. She would also have a letter correspondence with Ruth Graham, Billy Graham's wife as well as meeting their daughter Ann.

While Velma impressed the Christian do-gooders, the family members of the victims were not taken in by her "conversion."

"She's got religion now, they say," Margie Lee Pittman said. "Well, she had religion before. So we all thought."

A few more stays were granted until 1984 when the U.S. Supreme Court justice Warren Burger granted her a stay until August of that year. At this point, however, her execution seemed inevitable. In an ironic move, Velma would choose poison rather than the gas chamber and enjoyed the final visits from her children and grandchildren.

During the final week before her execution, the Reverend Hoyle, and his wife came to the prison with a battery-powered portable keyboard. His wife played the little organ then the Reverend sang "He Hideth My Soul" and "He is So precious to Me" in the cramped visitor booth.

Velma sang along, whistling in the graveyard before the reaper came for her.

She then wrote letters to each of the victim's family asking them for forgiveness. Reverend Hoyle would deliver the letters to the families, all of whom would refuse them.

MEET THE HANGMAN

As her execution date neared, Velma was placed in a solitary cell that stood directly across from the death chamber.

"It's total isolation," Velma said. "From everyone I had been with for six years."

North Carolina Governor James B.Hunt would reject her final plea for clemency.

On the day of her execution, the jail house would turn into a media frenzy. Death penalty advocates gathered outside the prison and chanted "Hip, hip, hurrah...K-I-L-L" while some sloganeered with "burn, bitch, burn". The protesters held up a few placards that quote Romans ch.13 which ironically was a verse that Velma would repeat to guards during her prison stay.

"For rulers are not a terror to good works, but to the evil...(The ruler) beareth no the sword in vain, for he is the minister of God, a revenger to execute wrath upon him that doeth evil."

The execution was scheduled to take place at 2:00 a.m but the protesters remained outside, their chants reduced to a simple "Kill her! Kill her!"

On November 2nd, 1984, Velma would be executed by lethal injection. The prison official came out and addressed the press, giving out copies of Barfield's statement of apology. The reporters then eagerly anticipated what Velma requested for her last meal. Initially, Velma just wanted the normally scheduled prison food; chicken livers, collard greens and a sheet cake with peanut butter icing. The last meal was delivered but Velma immediately lost her appetite. Instead, she opted for Cheese Doodles and a glass of Coca-Cola.

"Her attorney believed that Velma could have done some good in life," Orange said. "He stated that she could have become a teacher, counselor or a pastor. But her father set her on a path of self-destruction that she couldn't escape from. By the time she she left that road to ruin, she was too far gone in terms of her murderous acts. Justice had to be served in the end. In the end, the law doesn't care how genuine you are in your pleas for forgiveness. It only cares about the rule of law."

"I'm sorry for the hurt that I've caused," Velma said before her execution. "So many people, today if it were possible, I wish I could take every bit of hurt on myself."

KILLER CON WOMAN : THE TRUE STORY OF DEE DEE MOORE

SUSAN GRAHAM

Abraham Shakespeare didn't have too much going on in life. He was the son of an orange picker limited to menial day jobs. He never held a job where he made more than eight dollars an hour.

He didn't have a car, a driver's license or a credit card. He dropped out of school and could barely read or write.

The lanky 6'5" inch, 190 lbs laborer would patrol around town, looking for something to steal or people to assault.

He would go to jail two times and when he was released in 1995, he went to live with his mother.

Trying to cobble together any kind of life, Abraham would find work as a garbage man. Then he worked in a restaurant washing dishes before gaining employment on a shipping and receiving dock.

He was on the road to nowhere unless he hit the lottery.

On November 15th, 2006, however, he did just that. He rode shotgun with a truck driver named Michael Ford. They were making meat deliveries to restaurants in the area.

Ford then stopped off at the Town Star mini-mart in Frostproof. Abraham stayed in the car and Ford asked if he wanted anything.

Abraham only had ten dollars in his pocket. He asked for two quick picks in the lotto drawing.

Ford would buy the winning ticket for Abraham. The numbers 6, 12, 13, 34, 42, and 52 netted Abraham the $30 million dollar jackpot.

Ford would then sue him for what he believed should be "his share of the proceeds". He wanted no less than $1 million dollars and later claimed that Abraham had stolen the two tickets from his wallet.

"He knows the truth," Abraham said of Ford. "I know the truth."

The lawsuit hit the news wires but it took the jury only an hour to rule that Abraham did not steal the winning ticket from Ford's wallet.

"From my background investigation, he (Abraham) was always kind of a transient type," Ford's attorney, Michael Laurato, said. "If it wasn't for his criminal record, he kind of didn't exist."

Abraham would elect to take the lump sum cash payment of $17 million instead of the thirty annual payments totaling $30 million.

LET THE PARTY BEGIN

"Abraham was suddenly given the keys to the good life," Miami journalist Zack Jacobs said. "He threw a big party and suddenly found himself surrounded by numerous hangers-on. They partied and wined and dined. He paid them back for their attention with lavish gifts and cash prizes."

The first thing Abraham did was pay off his back child support which totaled almost $9,000. He then placed $1 million dollars into a trust fund for his son. He then gave his stepfather $1 million dollars and his three step-sisters $250,000 apiece. But his generosity didn't stop with his family. He paid off a $185,000 mortgage for a friend, $60,000 for another friend and another $53,000 for a mortgage for a man he had been "knowing for years."

Word of Abraham's open wallet began to spread.

His brother's best friend came over and he gave him $40,000. He gave his mother $12,000 and his sister $10,000.

In other words, he became the family ATM.

"Abraham's mother was the only one who grew wary of all of the well-wishers," Jacobs said. "She worked in a cafeteria at the local junior college and was a church-going woman. She thought that money was evil and was leery of Abraham getting so much of it. She knew that the folks coming around were just doing it out of their own selfish desires. They all wanted something from Abraham whereas before they wouldn't even give him the time of day."

Abraham would not heed his mother's warnings. He would write checks to whoever tugged at his heart strings. This meant paying for funerals of loved ones and people he didn't know.

"Abraham really had no idea of the value of money," Jacobs said. "And that isn't an insult. Remember, here was a guy who was in and out of jail. He never made more than eight dollars an hour. So, in his mind, seventeen million dollars would last forever. So, I think like most lottery winners, the initial euphoria simply consumed him. He was not thinking annuities and investments. He was simply enjoying all the indulgences and attention money could buy."

Abraham had other ideas about money.

"The Bible states it's better to give than to receive," Abraham said, explaining his gift giving.

Arnold Levine, another attorney who represented Ford in the suit, described Abraham as an "angry guy" whose made sure that his gifts came with "strings attached."

"My sense," Levine said, "was that some of his family members were unhappy with the amount of money he had parceled out to them. Were there people who were jealous? I would assume so."

After he gifted his relatives, Abraham began indulging himself. He purchased a Nissan Altima and a Rolex watch from a pawnshop. He then bought a 2006 F-150 pickup, a 2007 BMW 750i and finally a $1.1 million dollar home.

The brick and stucco home came replete with security cameras and a gate. It was over 6,500 square feet with an enclosed pool and a two two-car garages.

Aside from these extravagances, Abraham regretted winning the lottery. He was subject to constant requests for money from friends and even people he didn't know.

"I'd have been better off broke," Abraham later said to his brother. He then confided to another friend that "I thought all these people were my friends, but then I realized all they want is just money."

But Abraham only saw the tip of the iceberg. He was about to meet someone who didn't just want a little of his money. She wanted all of it.

And she was willing to kill him to get it.

Her name was Dorice Donegan Moore, better known as "Dee Dee".

ENTER THE CON

Dee Dee was a self-styled entrepreneur. A tall and shapely blonde, she was thirty-five years old and had a twenty-six-year-old boyfriend.

"Dee Dee was the kind of psychopath that could focus on her mark and not take no for an answer," Jacobs said. "She had an over the top, type-A personality. She could make her mark feel as if they were the only person in the world that mattered. She could look you straight in the eye and lie without any compunction."

She read about Abraham's story in the paper and the wheels in her head began to turn.

Dee Dee Morgan had tried to meet Abraham through his friends and even called his mother to no avail. Finally, she found out who sold him the million dollar estate, a realtor named Barbara Jackson.

"When I met her (Dee Dee), she was in a wheelchair," Jackson said. "She said she was in a car accident."

Dee Dee listened as Jackson told others about Abraham and how he changed their outlook about money. He insisted that it wasn't about money at all. It was about helping people. Jackson encouraged others to embrace this similar outlook.

Dee Dee feigned interest as she introduced herself to Jackson, telling the realtor that she was a writer. She said that she wanted to write an article or maybe even a book about Abraham, documenting his life so far and his viewpoints about money.

Jackson acquiesced and arranged for Dee Dee to meet Abraham.

"When she came to the house," Jackson said, "She jumped out of a Hummer, walking. And she was on heels. She said she healed herself through scuba therapy. It wasn't even two weeks."

Both Jackson and Abraham listened to Dee Dee's spiel. She spoke of her admiration for Abraham's philanthropy and wanted the world to hear about it.

Abraham was naïve and fell for the con. He agreed to have Dee Dee do the story about him.

"Abraham was vulnerable to someone with the manipulative charm of Dee Dee," Jacobs said. "Here was a guy who was about as down on his luck as you can get. Then he is a multi-millionaire overnight. He gets all the attention and love that was denied him his whole life. He really didn't know who to trust. Then along comes Dee Dee. She's well-spoken, well-dressed and seems to know what's going on inside his head."

What neither Abraham or Jackson didn't know was that Dee Dee Moore had a history of con artistry.

She had once staged a hoax that she believed would enable her to keep a Lincoln Navigator which was about to be repossessed. She had fallen hopelessly behind on the payments and had someone put the car in a garage. She then pretended that she was carjacked, kidnapped and raped by "three Mexican guys."

Dee Dee went all out in the pre-meditated scheme. She taped her wrists and threw herself out of someone else's moving car to make her injuries look real.

"This was an elaborate ruse," Jacobs said. "She had a friend drive her down the highway and she propelled herself out of the vehicle. She then tore apart her own clothes, smeared her make-up and started to cry. All of this was done as she crawled down the side of the highway, waiting for a sympathetic motorist to come pick her up."

A Good Samaritan would come along and take her to the hospital. She detailed her story to the police and medical staff, even going so far as to take a rape exam.

But her scheme was exposed and she would plead no contest to the charge and get probation. Always on the make for a new mark, Dee Dee needed another scheme. When she read about the lottery winning Abraham and his lawsuit with Ford, she had found herself a new patsy.

"Dee Dee couldn't make it on the straight road," Jacobs said. "Her businesses, whatever she was doing, were not generating any sufficient revenue for her to maintain the lifestyle that she felt she was entitled to. So she had to swindle and con. Unfortunately for Abraham, he got in her crosshairs."

LET'S START A BUSINESS

"Dee Dee was a master manipulator," Jacobs said. "She befriended Abraham first and gained his trust. She picked up on the fact that he had all of these people after his money. So she did some reverse psychology on him. She convinced Abraham that she was the opposite, that she would never take anything from him."

Convinced of Dee Dee's trustworthiness, Abraham agreed to start an LLC with the woman. They titled the business "Abraham Shakespeare LLC".

"He agreed to do this under the provision that anyone who asked for money would have to go through her," Jacobs said. "She convinced him that she had his best interests in mind. But in her mind, she saw him as a dupe. A rube. She was telling herself 'I'm going to work this guy. I'm going to work this guy and take everything he has. Schmuck!"

The corporation was in Abraham's name but the funds were under the control of Dee Dee.

Once she had control of the LLC, Dee Dee proceeded to withdraw $1 million dollars.

"She had totally hoodwinked poor Abraham," Jacobs said. "Now everything was under her own company banner, some type of bullshit medical company. Nothing came out of Abraham's account without her signature."

Abraham had stopped giving money to people without recompense. He then became the town ATM around his native Plant City. Judy Haggins helped him keep track of the loans as to who owed what.

Judy knew Abraham for fifteen years and she was taken aback that Dee Dee was involving herself in Abraham's affairs.

"When Abraham got ready to go to the bank one day to see about his money, (Moore) immediately called me on the phone," Judy said in the recording of her conversation with Smith. "You've got to stall him, Judy. He can't go to the bank."

Judy then received money from Abraham's account to pay for her help. "It was a little bit of money for me. (Moore) felt like Abraham should pay me to take his mama. Abraham used to come to me and say, 'Now you know that white woman got my money, she can do anything to me.' I said, 'Abraham, you can go get your money.'"

Judy could not stall Abraham, however. He drove over to Dee Dee's home to confront her. He wanted his money back under his name. All of it.

"It isn't working out," Abraham said. "I am going to the bank and straighten this shit out."

Dee Dee did her best to try and talk him out of it but Abraham was resolute in his decision.

"This was her worst fear come to light," Jacobs said. "Her mark had figured her out. Abraham was being nice about it but if he went to the bank there would be a huge investigation. She would go to jail. She couldn't let that happen."

Dee Dee would play along and told Abraham that she had all of his money in a safe she had behind her desk. She walked over to the safe and opened it.

But none of Abraham's money inside.

The only thing she had inside was a gun.

Spinning around, she pointed the pistol at Abraham.

"Aw shit," Abraham said. "Don't do it."

Dee Dee didn't listen. She fired twice, hitting Abraham in his chest, killing him. She then rolled up his body in a tarp and stole his cell phone.

"Her idea was to tap into people who owed Abraham money," Jacobs said. "She scanned through all of Abraham's text messages and realized how many people owed him money. Close to three million dollars. She figured she could impersonate him via cell phone messages and collect on these debts. An insane plan to any rational human being. But to do Dee Dee, a psychopath who thought she was smarter than everyone, it looked like easy money."

CLEANING UP THE MESS

Dee Dee contacted her ex-husband, James Moore to do some "yard work". She asked if he could dig a hole in her yard in April of 2009.

James could only scratch his head at the odd request.

"Why?" James asked.

"Oh, I just need a hole to bury some concrete and trash in," Dee Dee said. "I don't want my landlord to see all the stuff out here."

James would dig the hole then leave. But Dee Dee would call him back two hours later, however, asking him to fill the hole.

James, who was paid to do yard work by Dee Dee, agreed to fill the hole but didn't see what she had placed inside as it was now dark.

Dee Dee had placed Abraham's body in the hole.

A BLOOD TRAIL

Dee Dee continued to cover her tracks. She stole Abraham's cell phone and sent text messages to his family and friends, pretending to be the man she had just killed.

"Have to get away for awhile," Dee Dee texted Abraham's mother under his own cell phone number. "Going to the Caribbean."

The people receiving the texts became suspicious, however, because the texts didn't sound like him. Abraham was functionally illiterate. They would then text back for clarification and would be ignored. His mother grew especially worried. She texted back and told Abraham to call her.

His family now stalled, Dee Dee turned her attention to Abraham's assets. She used her own company, American Medical Professionals, to purchase Abraham's home.

In February of 2009, Dee Dee would purchase a 2008 Corvette for her boyfriend for $70,000. She would pay for this vehicle with a cashier's check from her American Medical Professionals, LLC business account.

"She had a boy toy," Jacobs said. "And she lavished the kid with money that she stole from Abraham. This included a house and a Corvette."

The following month, she purchased a 2009 Hummer for herself for $90,000 before taking her boy toy on a luxury vacation.

Abraham's family would report him missing on November 9th of 2009, almost seven months after his presumed date of death.

"Abraham told a friend that he was tired," Jacobs said. "He was tired of people constantly pressing him for money. So he hinted to more than one friend that he was 'fittin' to get outta here.' When no one saw him for a long period of time, they just wrote it off to the fact that he had gotten fed up with the situation and left town. It was only after they had not seen him for such a prolonged period of time that they finally reported it."

When questioned by police, Dee stated that Abraham left town. She said he was either in Texas, Jamaica, Puerto Rico, Florida or was admitted into a hospital.

"He was sick of people asking him for money," Dee Dee said. "I helped him leave town. He didn't tell me where he was going."

Dee Dee would state that the reason Abraham was taken off the account was because he didn't want to pay taxes. She couldn't give a reason for the fact that over $1 million was withdrawn only days after his name was taken off the LLC listing. She then said that Abraham also didn't want to pay child support.

Thinking she needed more accomplices, Dee Dee thought she could buy some. She approached the mother of one of Abraham's sons, telling her that she would give her a $200,000 house if she would lie to detectives and tell them that she had seen Abraham in recent days. She then paid a cousin of Abraham, Cedric Edom, over $5,000 to send his mother a birthday card and imply that it was from Abraham.

Abraham had not contacted his family since April of 2009. They believed that he was off on a Caribbean island somewhere enjoying his money.

"On a cruise," Dee Dee texted through Abraham's cell phone. "Having a great time."

But Abraham was far from the Jamaican isles. He was buried in five feet of dirt under a concrete slab.

LEAVING FINGERPRINTS BEHIND

Dee Dee sold her Hummer to a friend of a Chevrolet dealer for only $49,000. She said that she needed to get quick cash. Three weeks later, she had lunch with Elizabeth Walker, Abraham's mother.

Dee Dee also typed up a letter which she wanted to pass off as coming from Abraham.

"She had a brand-new laptop, set up and a printer, (and) she had a rubber-type gloves on," Abraham's friend, Gregory Smith recalled. "And a scarf pullover-type thing over her head."

'Don't worry about Dee,' the letter read. 'There are too many people that know I left. I gave her enough money... she would not take anything from me unless I agreed.'

She then had Gregory call Abraham's mother and pretend he was Abraham.

"Hi Mom," Gregory said. "I'm fine. Had to get away."

"Who is this?" Elizabeth said. "You're not Abe! Who are you?"

Dee Dee made her first strategic error here. Elizabeth Walker knew her son's voice and the voice on the other end did not belong to him. She contacted police who investigated and eventually caught up with Gregory Smith.

Gregory would cooperate and play informant against Dee Dee. This would involve the use of an undercover police officer to aid Gregory.

Dee Dee had told Gregory that she needed someone to take the fall for Abraham's murder. She told Gregory to find someone that would accept $50,000 in exchange for declaring themselves guilty of Abraham's murder. Gregory told the investigators of the scheme and they had an undercover cop, Mike Smith, come along with Gregory as they arranged a deal.

"I did it (help the undercover operation) because when they explained to me what was going on and they said they had their suspicions that something like I told them," Gregory Smith said. "He had money. He could have went anywhere. Anybody was saying anything. I didn't know where he was, really didn't go into where he was. But the deal is when they came to me and they explained to me that there was an investigation going on. And I wouldn't get in no trouble and I could walk out of there right now, but they needed some help to find Abraham. I said I'd see what I could do. "

Dee Dee met with the undercover officer. The con artist was about to be conned.

"The undercover officer explained himself as someone up on federal charges," Jacobs said. "He was about to be sent to jail for life. He could take the $50,000 and live it up in his final days. But what he needed from Dee Dee was proof that he was the killer."

Dee Dee took the bait. She showed the undercover detective where she had buried Abraham, five feet under a concrete slab in her backyard.

"I need you to dig him up," Dee Dee said. "And then burn his body."

She also gave the undercover cop the gun that was used to kill Abraham.

"She gave Mike the map of her backyard," Jacobs said. "She was so blinded by her own need to get away with the crime that she didn't she that she was being played. He was wired up the whole time. They had everything they needed on tape. She confessed to everything."

"Don't forget to bring the marshmallows," Dee Dee said to the undercover cop when she told him to burn Abraham's body.

EXCAVATING THE BODY

Digging at the site, the police unearthed Abraham's body. They then brought Dee Dee back in for another interrogation.

The con woman would give them multiple stories. First, she said that drug dealers killed Abraham. Then it was his attorney that had him killed. Then she would blame her fourteen-year-old son before finally saying that she killed Abraham herself...but only in self-defense.

Dee Dee's manipulations didn't stop there.

She told one of the investigating detectives, David Clark, that she hoped they could eventually have sex once the investigation was over.

"I find you very attractive," Dee Dee said to Clark.

Detectives would estimate that Abraham died around April 6th or 7th. They would take Dee Dee into custody and charge her with accessory to murder.

"The money was like a curse to him," Dee Dee said to reporters. "And now it's become a curse to me. God knows I would never take another human being's life."

COURTROOM DRAMA

During the trial, Dee Dee began making threats to jurors. Two of the jurors would state that Gregory Smith had intimidated them in the parking lot. Smith, a convicted felon five times over, denied the charges. The judge would ask one of the jurors if she had felt threatened by Dee Dee or any members of her family or friends and the juror simply responded that she wanted to feel safe.

The judge would then caution Dee Dee from making 'facial expressions' at the jurors as she would stare stone-faced at some of them, trying to intimidate.

The jury would deliberate for three hours before finding Moore guilty of the first-degree murder charge.

"She got every bit of his money," Assistant State Attorney Jay Pruner said. "He found out about it and threatened to kill her. She killed him first."

Dee Dee's attorney Byron Hileman argued otherwise, stating that there were other suspects that the prosecution should have went after.

"There were a lot of people who owed Mr. Shakespeare a lot of money," Hileman said. "One guy owed him a million dollars. The police focused on Dee Dee Moore and they didn't even consider other people."

Judge Emmett Battles called Dee Dee "the most manipulative person I have ever seen" and that she was "cold, calculating and cruel."

Dee Dee Moore would be convicted of first-degree murder on December 20th, 2012.

She would be sentenced to life in prison without the possibility of parole with an additional 25 years.

"'I'm missing my little brother," Abraham's brother Robert Brown said after the proceedings. "What ain't gonna be back no more. Dead and gone, and everything. He ain't coming back."

Dee Dee maintains that she is innocent and that her trial did not have evidence that would have exonerated her. She states that she is writing two books as well as penning poetry.

"Friends are a gift,

You give yourself.

When life has too many,

Mountains to climb alone." - Dee Dee Moore

KIM SNIBSON : MASTER MANIPULATOR

SARAH BOSWELL

"Why is this happening?"

Those may have been Greg Hosa's last audible words as Andrew Flentjar and Stacy Lea-Caton brutally forced him to the ground. The answer Flentjar gave would shock not just Hosa, but both of his attackers. For it was that response that would have allowed both Flentjar and Lea-Caton to realize that they were not part of the just cause they had believed themselves to be, but were in fact at the mercy of Kim Snibson's deluded and volatile plan.

Kim Snibson is a master manipulator who was envious of the life Greg Hosa and his wife Kathryn McKay had built together. Most notably, their horse farm. Situated in Nowra, New South Wales, Champagne Shires would be considered a small property when compared to the amount of land horse farms usually covered. Still, despite its modest size, it was far grander that Snibson could ever hope to own herself. For her, Champagne Shires was the perfect combination of all her fondest desires and life passions. Living next door to her dream made reality, it didn't take long for her fantasies of owning the property to become a perceived right. Snibson's greed led her to believe that she deserved Champagne Shires, while her ego convinced her that she could have it, if only the current owners were dealt away with.

Once Hosa and McKay had agreed to stable her horse, Snibson had the perfect excuse to visit her neighbors. She would come by often and grew to know both Hosa and McKay well. This access only fuelled her lust for the property and her disdain for the happy owners. Unaware of Snibson's feelings towards them, Hosa and McKay remained kind and generous to their neighbor. On one known occasion, Snibson had fallen behind in payments and owed the couple $300 for the care of her horse. Hosa and McKay had agreed to continue to stable her horse and told Snibson that she could pay them when she was able. This generosity did not provoke gratitude in Snibson, but instead fed into her increasing resentment. By this time she had begun to believe that she could force the couple to sign over the rights to Champagne Shires to her, kill them, and live happily on the property without consequence. Rationally this plan is ludicrous, but given her past success, Snibson believed it to be perfect.

Years earlier Snibson had inherited her house in Calymea Street, Nowra Hill, from an elderly woman named Judith Plankas. It was this property that had made her a neighbor of Hosa and McKay, and ultimately, it was in this house that the couple would be murdered. But it wasn't until after her arrest that questions began to arise as to exactly why and how Ms Plankas came to deed the property to Snibson.

In an interview with Take-5 Magazine, Snibson's ex-husband recalled how Ms Snibson had befriended Ms Plankas. At the time, the elderly dog breeder had been diagnosed with cancer and had needed help taking care of her animals. Snibson had been quick to offer assistance and for a while must have struck the sickly Ms Plankas as a Godsend. But, as Mr Snibson told Take-5 Magazine, "Kim got hold of powerful tranquilizers and quietly killed the older dogs." Perhaps accustomed to Kim's crueler actions, or blinded by devotion, it is believed that Mr Snibson neglected to inform Plankas of what Kim had done. By all appearances, Ms Plankas had no idea what kind of woman she had welcomed into her home.

"Then on April 17, 2003," Mr Snibson recalled, "Judith's condition suddenly worsened. She changed her will that night, leaving the house to Kim, and died the next day."

This would not be the first time Mr Snibson had been privy to the threat Kim posed to those around her. And it would not be the only time his failure to believe or act lead to disastrous consequences. In the same interview, he revealed a conversation he had once had with a woman named Rebecca. She had only been 15-years-old when Ms Snibson had convinced her to move out of the home and in with the Snibson family.

"We've got a free babysitter," Ms Snibson had announced when she had brought the teenager home, according to her ex-husband. He went on to say that, "later, Rebecca sought me out and what she had to say rocked me. Kim had kept a horse at a stable owned by an elderly couple and Rebecca said (that Kim) talked about tying them up, making them sign over their property to her and killing them."

Still, it would seem that Mr Snibson was not then willing to believe his wife capable of such things. But Rebecca wasn't Snibson's first nor only attempt at recruiting accomplices in her murder plot. Nor was the teenager's confession the only one to be dismissed. Armed with vicious lies and a willingness to manipulate all those around her, Snibson approached numerous people. Perhaps it is a testament to her skill at manipulation, or her ability to choose those reluctant to cause a stir without any solid evidence, but many of the people she approached never spoke of the conversations until after she had been arrested. Mr Snibson claimed that was when he began to receive calls from dozens of friends, most of which started with 'I've been wanting to tell you this for years'.

"Then they'd tell me about an affair she'd had or how she'd tried to enlist them in a desperate scheme to have someone beaten up or killed," he told Take-5 Magazine. He also spoke about how a friend had told him that 'Kim had wanted an old lady beaten up because she said her son had molested one of your girls'. "Nobody has touched my daughters," Mr Snibson said. "It was a fantasy made up by Kim to get others to do terrible things for her."

With so many people aware of the true, malicious nature of Snibson, it is baffling how few people voiced their concerns to law enforcement. Snibson continued her search for willing participants until she found two men who believed her lies. Her first recruit was Andrew Flentjar. He was a neighbor of the Snibson family, although Mr Snibson insists that he didn't know Flentjar that well, and had believed that Snibson hadn't either.

"She didn't socialize with (him) or stay for a cuppa," he had said in an interview. But still Snibson had managed to make the otherwise reasonable man willing to help her in her plan to kidnap and assault Mr Hosa.

"Andrew was told by Kim that the couple had sexually abused her child and had videoed the episode," Paul Leask, a Crown Prosecutor for New South Wales, reviled on the television show Deadly Women.

In her interview on the same television show, a journalist for Illawarra Mercury Newspaper, Veronica Apap, attested that there had been "no evidence at any time in court that Kathryn or Greg had engaged in anything like that." Still, Flintjar believed the story Snibson wove and, under the impression that her plan only involved minor assault as justice for her daughter, agreed to help.

Snibson then approached Stacy Lea-Caton, a former neighbor who had been in trouble with the law. Mr Snibson remembers Lea-Caton as being a man who continuously worked to create a notable reputation for himself as a dangerous man.

"You would be talking about normal things," Mr Snibson told Ms Apap during an interview, "and Stacey would come in with something bigger or better. He talked about his criminal history, stuff like that."

Mr Snibson went on to say that when it came to Mr Lea-Caton he "didn't believe anything he told me", and that, "I didn't think he would go very well in a fight, myself. He is not this tough person he was making himself out to be."

Ms Snibson, however, saw a potential for violence in Lea-Caton and knew just how to bring it to the surface. During a visit she tested the waters by telling him a lie similar to the one she had recruited Flintjar with. According to Leask, "Stacey Lea-Caton was told by her that the couple had drugged her, sexually assaulted her, and videoed the episode."

Once again there she could produce any evidence in support of her claims, nor could later investigators. According to Apap, "It seems to be a total fantasy on her part" and Mr Snibson has stated that "Greg Hosa was a thoroughly decent person who did not deserve such terrible lies to be made up about him, let alone die so needlessly." Still, Snibson was convincing enough to for Lea-Coton to push aside his desire to get his life back on track and he soon found himself alongside Flintjar, embroiled in Snibson's supposed plan for vigilante justice.

"She employed a means of modulating the story depending on the person who was the recipient of it. To press the right buttons." Leask asserted. "The theme was always one of sexual impropriety and of course, nothing excites people's sympathy more than that."

With her two accomplices waiting for instructions, Snibson put her plan into action on January 28th, 2006. It was easy to lure Hosa to her home. The 56-year-old man didn't suspect that anything might be wrong when Snibson called and asked him to come over.

"He came quickly after that conversation occurred," Apap said in her Deadly Women interview. "He didn't think that he was in any danger or that there would be any problem."

Lea-Carton and Flintjar swarmed Hosa as he entered the Snibson home. Using a slab of wood they struck him on the head and forced him to the ground. The men then proceeded to hogtie Hosa, forcing him onto his stomach and binding his legs to his hands. It was during this attack that Hosa asked his assailants "why is this happening?" While the exact wording cannot be determined, it is reported that Flintjar responded by accusing Hosa of pedophilia.

With this declaration both of Snibson's henchmen realized that they had been lied to. They were blindsided by the revelation yet, having participated in assault and kidnapping, and still unaware of just how malicious Snibson's intentions were, neither felt they were in a position to leave. Snibson deceit had taken them past the point of no return and both were at a loss at what to do next. This afforded Snibson the perfect environment to maintain control.

While the men watched over a struggling Hosa, Snibson called his wife and 'confessed' that she and Hosa had been having an affair. It was a story that few would believe and later would be seen by their family as adding a foul insult to considerable injury. Jan Keily, a sister of McKay, would attest that they family was 'disgusted' by the claim. But on that night, it was enough to draw McKay into Snibon's trap.

Just like her husband, 44-year-old McKay was set upon by Lea-Carton and Flintjar. She too was hogtied and gagged by having a sock forced into her mouth and taped into place. Once again the men found themselves forced into a situation far from what they had been expecting when Snibson left to retrieve two 44-gallon drums from Champagne Shires and brought them to the house.

After shoving Ms McKay into one of the drums Snibson disclosed the needlessly cruel method she had chosen in order to kill McKay. "She murdered Kathryn by wrapping tape around her face and eyes and nose," Leask described.

Many factors must be considered when determining how long it would take an individual to suffocate to death. First, oxygen deprivation renders the victim unconscious. If they are still unable to breath brain damage will begin. As a general guide, it is believed to take approximately 5-6 minutes for death to occur. Snibson, Lea-Carton, and Flintjar stood by and watched McKay struggle for this entire length of time. When arrested, all three would give varying statements as to what exactly had happened that night, but in all versions, the two men who had not agreed to murder still made no attempt to save Ms McKay.

When Snibson turned her attention back to Hosa, she had a different method in mind for his execution. According to Leask, "Kim killed Greg Hosa by garrotting him with electrical wire. Kim killed them both deliberately and methodically." And once again, her now reluctant accomplices failed to put an end to her actions.

As night fell the trio loaded the two barrels, each now filled with the corpses of a once loving couple, into the back of Snibson's truck. Together the three drove to a remote patch of the Tomerong State Forest. Here she doused the remains of Ms McKay and Mr Hosa with petrol and set them alight.

As Leask stated, "Incinerating the bodies was done for no other purpose than to destroy evidence that those two poor people had ever been to Kim's house that day."

For all her obsession and manipulation, it took only hours for Snibson's plan to come undone. As it would turn out, Mr Snibson's reading of Stacey Lea-Caton's character had been far more reliable that Kim's had been. The only known criminal within the trio, Lea-Carton was unable to suppress his guilty conscious and within hours of leaving Snibson confessed to his sister and her husband. The series of events he told them had been highly edited but it was still damning enough that the young couple had insisted that he tell the authorities. At 2:30am they had taken him to the Nowra Police Station to report the crime. According to police, Lea-Caton had originally stated that he had seen a man and woman tried up at the farm and was worried that they might come to harm. By 8:00am they had arrested Snibson. A whole day hadn't passed by the time police located the remains of Greg Hosa and Kathryn McKay. Superintendent Kyle Stewart would describe the discovery as a "horrific scene", while Leask provided greater detail. "All that remained of Kathryn was her right foot and little remained of Greg."

But even when caught Snibson was far from willing to admit to her actions. In her statements to the police, she was a hapless witness to a domestic disturbance that spiraled out of control. According to Snibson, she had informed Ms McKay that she had been having an affair with Mr Hosa. Hosa had come to her home first, followed by and enraged Ms McKay. Once there, the couple had begun to argue. The confrontation soon grew volatile and in the heat of the moment Lea-Caton had picked up a bird perch and struck Mr Hose over the head hard enough that he fell to the ground. She recounted how this hadn't deterred Ms McKay who had then turned her anger onto Snibson herself. McKay had become so furious that she had 'come at' Snibson. This had forced Flentjar, who had also happened to be present, to tackle the older woman to keep her from harming Snibson.

"She fell back and hit her head on the pantry and fell on the floor," Snibson told police. She further went on to explain that is was after Ms McKay had been injured that Lea-Caton's murderous intent rose to the surface. In Snibson's version of events, it was Lea-Caton that strangled Hosa with a rope before forcing her to wrap tape around McKay's head until, as she insisted he had instructed, 'she turned blue'. In his final act of depravity, Lea-Caton had been the one to light the bodies on fire.

Her behavior at the trials of her accomplices was a far cry from what others had observed during her own trial. While giving evidence in the New South Wales Supreme Court, Snibson broke down into tears as she described the "gurgling sounds" Mr Hosa made as the life was choked out of him. Snibson would tell the court that she felt "sick to my stomach" about the murders. She continued to say that she thought about it "every single day." She had become so unsettled that Justice Terence Buddin had to adjourn the sentencing hearing for five minutes to give her time to compose herself.

Compared to her behavior and demeanor at other times it was almost possible to believe Ms Snibson was two entirely different people. For Leask, there was no doubt which persona was ligament and which she put on for self-preservation.

"There will be no remorse from Kim Snibson. It's not in her nature," he had said in an interview. He also claimed that Snibson is a person "that lacks the quality that makes us human beings." But perhaps his opinion on Snibson was most elegantly and directly described within his statement, "I have been involved in some shocking crimes involving some dreadful brutality. This case stands out because, in my career, I can only reasonably expect to come across one or two sociopaths. And that's what Kim Snibson is."

It is a sentiment echoed by Candice DeLong, a former criminal profiler for the Federal Bureau of Investigation who often lends her insights to programs such as Deadly Women. "It's unlikely Kim feels remorse for what she did. Sociopaths never do," she said during an interview. She further asserted that "if she ever does emerge from prison, watch out."

It is DeLong's opinion that "Kim is a natural born killer. She wanted to commit murder," but for those like her ex-husband, Snibson is not so clearly an evil woman. While he called her 'pure evil' in an interview with Take-5

Magazine it was also discovered that he had withheld information from investigators in a bid to protect her from prosecution.

"I did tell the truth in all statements," he told the New South Wales Supreme Court. "I left out those couple of sentences from Kim because it sounded very damning to me. I didn't want to see anything bad happen to her. I still had loyalty to Kim even though we had long broken up."

Some of these omitted sentences referred to statements Ms Snibson had made the day after her arrest. According to Mr Snibson, she had said "Don't worry about me, I'm a bad person", and had alluded that she would be 'going away' for 30 years. He further stated that Snibson had said that while she did want to tell him what had happened on the night of the murders her lawyer had instructed her not to talk about it. "She said when she gets to court and has her say, the truth will come out."

Whether Mr Snibson truly believes in his ex-wife's innocence or not, he unwittingly brought more evidence against her. When Detective Sergeant Jason Hogan had asked Mr Snibson to take them to where he as Ms Snibson used to train their dogs for dog sled competitions he had agreed. The location he had led them to had been the where the smoldering barrels holding the remains of McKay and Hosa had been found. In the same day, he had also unknowingly brought the police to the part of Braidwood Road where Mr Hosa's burnt out four-wheel drive had been discovered.

Andrew Wayne Flentjar was the first to be sentenced. He is currently serving a minimum of 10-years for his role in assisting in the kidnapping of Hosa and McKay. Stacey Lea-Caton pleaded guilty to aiding and abetting murder and received a sentence of a minimum 16 years, with the maximum time served of 22-years.

Lea-Caton testified against Snibson during her trail and put a great amount of pressure on her supposed version of events. Combined with the sight of the 44-gallon drums, similar to those used to dispose of McKay and Hosa's remains, which were brought into the courtroom, the cracks in Snibson's account of that night were beginning to show. Whatever the 10 men and 2 women of the jury had truly believed was rendered moot when, approximately halfway through her trial, Snibson changed her plea to guilty.

On September 5th, 2008 Snibson faced her sentencing hearing. By Australian law, those affected by a crime have the right to lodge and read out a victim impact statement to the court and the perpetrator. The friends and family of Hosa and McKay took advantage of this opportunity. Marion, Katheryn McKay's sister, described how the murders had rendered her family into a state similar to 'animals caught in headlights'. In her statement, she explained how she struggled "to find the words for the numbness and traumatic feelings the murders caused the family."

Marion described the impact of their loss and Snibson's actions as being felt "physically, socially, emotionally and psychologically." How her family is no longer able to watch programs about horses or the news, as they stir up too many painful memories. How her work as a counselor has suffered and that the majority of her grief-stricken family has since abandoned their homes in Nowra.

She described McKay and Hosa as loving, community-minded people, and reminded the court and Snibson that her sister had been a nurse with a natural drive and desire to help other people. She reiterated how their senseless and brutal deaths have had a lasting impact on hundreds of other people and how more than 500 people had attended their funerals. Somewhere within this speech, Kim Snibson reportedly began to cry.

Another of McKay's sisters, Jan Keily, spoke of her utter confusion at how Snibson, Flintjar, and Lea-Caton could have brought themselves to do what they had done. She also addressed how insulting it was to the memories or their loved ones that Snibson still maintained that there had been an affair, not to mention the accusations she had made about McKay's intended violence towards Snibson. "The families are shocked by the lies that have been told about Kathryn McKay and Gregory Hosa by the three offenders."

Justice Buddin commended the sisters for the dignity and grace they had shown while delivering their statements before adjourning the proceedings. When he delivered the final verdict, Justice Buddin gave his own opinion on the case before him. He expressed how the crimes against this kind-hearted couple had been committed with a "considerable degree of callousness".

Justice Buddin explored the suffering that was inflicted upon Mr Hosa and Ms McKay, not just at the agonizingly slow and painful death, but at the mental torture that must have endured at the hands of the captors. He expressed how they were forced to wait for a "not inconsiderable amount of time", stuck in a state of anguish, wondering what their kidnappers would decide to do to them. "They were totally defenseless and at the mercy of the offenders," he said.

Justice Buddin then turned his attention to the version of events that Snibson had put forth, the version of events that left her as a victim of circumstances and Lea-Coton's vicious nature. He described this story as "implausible", "quite fanciful" and "tailored to suit inescapable, objective facts". As proof of the ridiculousness of her claims, he pointed to her recruitment of accomplices. This was not an act of a woman caught off guard by a lover's spat but instead was indicative of the level of calculation and manipulation she was capable of wilfully wielding.

While Snibson had told the court that she was sorry for the role she had played in the couple's grizzly end, Justice Buddin was not swayed. He explained that he had not believed her words to be those of someone truly remorseful and repentant, but instead said that whatever contrition she had expressed struck him as contrived. His final verdict had been a jail sentence of no less than 32 years. This means that Snibson would be 60-years-old before she becomes eligible to apply for parole.

The town of Nowra is still healing from the horrors of that singular night. As Paul Leask has stated, "that one of their own was the killer was something that psychologically traumatized that community." The senseless cruelty Snibson brought down upon a devoted, generous couple has only been magnified by the ridiculousness of her plan. For all the action she was willing to take there was no way her plan would allow her to gain ownership of Champagne Shire, rendering her depraved actions useless and her goal unattainable.

But perhaps what is hardest for the residents of Nowra, and all that hear of the tragic deaths of McKay and Hosa, to come to terms with, is the wealth of opportunities presented for people to intervene. Be it out of embarrassment or social delicacy, those who had concerns over Sibson's actions had refused to disclose what they had known. At the time it might have been dismissed as a personal eccentricity, a misunderstanding, or a benign threat, but now blaze as warning signs for the brutality that was to come. Perhaps if those who had felt the inkling of concern had stepped forward a different course could have been plotted and McKay and Hosa could have been spared. But then it is also possible that nothing could have deterred Snibson, and that these murders were the only end her insatiable greed would have allowed. Wherever the truth may lie, it is too late to act for McKay and Hosa. Their lives have already been sacrificed on the altar of Snibson's pride. The only solace that is to be garnished now is that Snibson has been removed from the general population and will hopefully be unable to claim any further victims. But what little comfort this offers will forever be overshadowed by the influence Snibon's name will forever provoke. Those who learn about the merciless crimes this woman visited upon the people who would have been her friends will undoubtedly no longer be able to look at their neighbors without there being the lingering question of 'what if?'

THE DEFRANCISCO SISTERS

64

KORI MAYER

CHAPTER ONE

Regina and Margaret DeFrancisco are two sisters convicted of first degree murder.

On paper, the two sisters look like two girls you would see at a church social.

In school, both were good but not great students. Margaret was the pretty one. She would get all of the attention from the boys but return little interest.

Margaret was a student at Jones College Prep School, a selective public institution that is considered one of the top high schools in Illinois.

A little on the shy side, Margaret had a quick wit and sense of humor. Sweet-looking and pretty, she had avoided any kind of trouble throughout her young life. Her early photos suggest, however, that her subtle smirk was a couldn't contain the narcissism that was growing within.

"You would look at Margaret and see right through her," one of her neighbors said. "It was black, like was nothing there. She didn't seem like she had depth, like she had compassion."

Regina had a love for animals, particularly ponies. She rode horses and in her words, "never lost a show."

Regina was also the more extroverted of the two, wearing her emotions on her sleeve. She could mouth off and had a chip on her shoulder. She also had a thing for 'bad boys', seeing them as a reflection of herself.

"A lot of girls get turned on by the 'thug life'," forensic psychologist Marnie Clark said. "The DeFrancisco sisters definitely fit that mold. They were not out to play Mrs. Cleaver when they grew up. They were attracted to the gang lifestyle. They thought the drama was exciting."

The girls were raised by a single parent, Nora DeFrancisco. Nora raised the two sisters and their brother Joey in the Pilsen neighborhood of Chicago. Their father, Augie DeFrancisco was a small-time burglar and convicted drug dealer who had no involvement in the girl's childhood years. Their maternal grandfather, Gilbert Smith, was a former Chicago cop who was fired from the force in 1960 after admitting that he was "friendly with certain burglars."

Growing up in Pilsen, however, the girls could not avoid rubbing shoulders with gang members. They became enamored with gang culture, learning who fought against who and what the names of the gangs were. There were the Latin Counts, Kool Gang, Villa Lobos, Bishops, among many other offshoots. The girls knew what streets signified what gang members' territory and memorized their hand signals.

"Chicago is simply rife with gangs," Clark said. "It is inescapable, even to those in the more affluent communities. There is still a choice, however. For whatever reason, the DeFrancisco sisters were drawn to the 'thug life'. To a young person, it looks 'cool'. They are the classic examples of young women who could not see the big picture and thought the thug life was something worth aspiring to."

The two sisters, with their striking brunette looks, could not help but come into the cross hairs of the local gang members. They began wearing dark lipstick and teasing their hair out. Margaret would get a tattoo on her belly. Regina would have the letter "R" tattooed on her leg as well as a drawing of a heart just above her breast. They would hang out on street corners and in front of the local liquor store, chatting up the neighborhood 'gangstas'.

"The changes in their make-up and dress signified the changes in their personality," Clark said. "They grew bored during their time at prep school. Even ashamed. They did not want to see themselves as nerds and hated that aspect of themselves. Starting in eighth grade, it was time to start rebelling. By the time they reached high-school, the thug life was part of their persona. Dark make-up. Tattoos. Hanging out with gang bangers. Alcohol and drugs. But most important, they wanted all the drama that came with that kind of life. Who is out to get who, who dissed who and who shot who became their modus operandi in life."

Grandfather Gilbert, however, had seen this all before as a Chicago cop. He feared that the girls, particularly Regina, would become ensnared by the street gang culture. He tried to obstruct this from happening and found Regina a job with a local periodontist. He figured if he kept the girl busy with school and work it would keep her away from the idiots on the street.

Regina, however, did not have the emotional maturity to see the light. She showed up late for her first couple of shifts then she was fired.

But she had started dating a man named Johnny Rivera, a known member of Chicago's notorious "Latin Kings" street gang. Rivera had a rap sheet as long as "War and Peace" as well as more aliases than a Russian spy

Regina would learn how to package and deal drugs at the foot of Johnny. She would watch him put the cocaine into plastic bags, measuring it out by the ounce. They would drive around town and Johnny would introduce her to his customers, watching as he conducted the deals. The secret handshakes and secret lingo all became apart of Regina's world.

Officially crossing over from innocent prep school girl to drug dealing girlfriend, Regina lived a double life. She did manage to get a part-time job doing data entry work for a local law firm and had enrolled in the local junior college (Harold Washington).

Margaret was getting into trouble as well. Her grades in high school were slipping as she would sneak out at night to be with friends. She would often come to school looking "disheveled" according to one teacher who thought she looked like a child whose parents were going through a divorce.

And there was trouble on the home front.

Neighbors would report hearing the girls fighting with their mother on a daily basis.. The two girls were out of control with no father figure to put them in line. Nora would berate Regina whenever she would act up in school or get arrested and the girls would yell back.

In private, Nora would refer to her daughters as "the bitches".

Things would come to a head when Regina would get arrested for selling cocaine to an undercover cop. A single mom already strapped for cash as she had to support three children on her own, Nora was livid as she paid Regina's bail.

"How are you going to pay me back?" .

"I don't know!"

"Do you know how much it costs to bail you out of jail!" Nora screamed. "You are going to pay me back. You're going to pay me back every penny!"

CHAPTER TWO

"She needs money," Margaret said, her voice full of concern.

"How much?" Oscar asked.

"One thousand dollars. Can you help us out, baby?"

That was the scene set for the twenty-two year old Oscar Velazquez in June of 2000 as he spoke to the sister of his current teenage crush, Regina DeFrancisco. He spotted Regina around the neighborhood of Pilsen and quickly fell for her dark Irish-Italian good looks. Showing off his brand new Z28 Camaro, he chatted up the girls before he asked Regina out for tacos. The two began going out but Regina didn't like him...at first. Then she realized that he had some money and was all too willing to spend it on her.

"Oscar wasn't the typical guy that Regina would go for," Clark said. "Regina liked the 'bad boy', the thug. Oscar wasn't in street gang culture. He had immigrated from Mexico and actually had a real job, earning his living the old fashioned way as a truck driver. If anything, Regina would see someone like him as a sucker, someone who she could use."

Still, Regina was what Oscar wanted. He persisted in calling her, asking when he could see her again.

"He's a creepy guy," Regina told her sister, Margaret as her cell phone rang. She looked at the caller ID. Yep, it was Oscar.

"But maybe you can get some money from him?"

"Here, you talk to him," Regina said handing the cell phone to Margaret. "Just make up some baloney that I'm in jail or something."

"What?"

"Get rid of him. Tell him I need bail money."

"Hello, Oscar?" Margaret answered the phone.

"Yeah," Oscar said. "Who is this?"

"It's Margaret," she said, sounding as if she was trying to stifle tears. "Regina is in jail. She's locked up."

"What?"

"They put her in jail for something she didn't even do. They want one thousand dollars. One thousand dollars to bail her out."

Margaret smiled like a devil at her sister.

"I can help," Oscar said.

"No," Margaret said, sniffling. "It's too much."

"It's for your sister."

Oscar would persist in his willingness to help out, however. Margaret played him like a violin, agreeing to meet with Oscar to take his hard earned money.

"Oscar gave Margaret the money in the hopes of scoring points with the sisters," Clark said. "He thought that by being 'nice' and bailing them out of trouble they would find him attractive. Instead, it just fueled their contempt for him. These girls liked thugs. Bums. They cared little for Oscar's chivalry."

Regina would not use the money to pay back her mother, however. She would give the money to her real boyfriend, Johnny, who bought an "old school ride" car with Oscar's money.

Oscar would call Regina over twenty-four times during the next five days wanting to know what happened. He began to feel like the sucker he was.

He had a wife and kids in Mexico. But here in Chicago he fell for the brown-haired beauty and became all too willing to be her patsy.

"Oscar was playing with fire," Clark said. "He just didn't realize how far gone the girls were in terms of narcissism. He didn't see the fact that they didn't even see him as a human being. All he saw was batting eyelashes and pretty faces. He was totally smitten with Regina despite the fact that he had a wife and kids back in Mexico. Here he was, in Chicago, where he was free from the responsibilities of family. He could have a little fun and if he had to spend some money to do it, so be it."

CHAPTER THREE

The two sisters were surprised at how easy it was to extract money out of Oscar. With one fake phone call, they had one thousand dollars cash to their name.

"They were both attractive girls in the neighborhood," Clark said. "They were young, looking up to gang members and drug dealers for the power they had. But the girls realized that they had their own power. The power of budding sexuality that could make men do what they wanted. They could trick men into doing things for them with a future promise of sex."

Oscar continued to call and it would be only a matter of time before he would be confronted with the truth that he had been lied to. The girls had to construct a plan to get rid of him.

"I have an idea," Margaret said, picking up the cell phone and calling their fifteen year old friend, Veronica Garcia.

"Need your help," Margaret said as Veronica picked up.

"For what?" Veronica asked.

"I need a gun. Can you get a gun?"

"A gun?"

"Can your boyfriend get a gun?"

Veronica, like the DeFrancisco sisters, was enamored with street gang members. She had a boyfriend who could obtain whatever you needed, drugs or guns.

"Why?"

"We're going to stick up and rob Oscar," she said.

"You're not going to kill him are you?"

"We're just going to scare him a little," Margaret laughed.

Veronica did as she was asked, getting a gun from her boyfriend and heading straight over to the DeFrancisco sister's home.

"Nice," Margaret said, looking the pistol over, closing one eye as she looked through the cross hairs. "So where we going to do this?"

"Right here," Regina said, waving her hands around the living room.

"No way," Margaret said. "If the neighbors complain about us screaming and yelling then they're going to hear a gunshot. Duh."

Regina looked around the home. The basement door caught her eye.

"We'll lead him down there," Regina said, leading her sister down the basement steps. "Nobody can hear anything down here. The noise will be drowned out."

"Here," Margaret said, removing some blue tarp from the shelf. She spread the material down on the basement floor in front of the steps. "We can't leave any blood stains."

"Check you out," Regina laughed. "Miss Perry Mason."

Margaret laughed as she flattened out the tarp, placing it in a perfect line with the basement stairs. "Okay," she said, walking halfway up the steps. "So if we shoot him from here," pointing her forefinger into a gun. "He'll fall straight down there."

"Perfect."

The two sisters giggled and gave each other fist bump.

"Here is where the disconnect took place," Clark said. "They had embraced an environment and a culture where there were a lot of faux tough guys. Guys who said they would commit violence but for the most part it was all talk. The girls took it literally. At no point did they realize the gravity of what they were doing. They wanted to be 'gangstas', they wanted to be seen as 'hard'. They didn't have the maturity or the experience to realize that all of those 'gangstas' that they look up to are in jail. They didn't see Oscar at all. He was less than human. Something that is used, discarded and desecrated when it is no longer of use."

CHAPTER FOUR

Oscar was surprised that Regina finally called him back.

"Hey," she said, her teenaged voice soft and inviting.

"You're out of jail?" he asked.

"Yeah," she said. "I really appreciate what you did for me. That was really sweet of you."

"No worries," he said. "I need my money back. Been calling you like crazy."

"I'm sorry, I've just been busy."

"Yeah, I understand. But I need my money back."

"I was wondering if there was some other way I can pay you back?" she said in a sensual tone of voice.

"Like?"

"Like, I know you think my sister is hot, right?"

"What's that got to do with anything?"

"It is something we've been thinking about," she said. "But if you're not cool with it, it's okay."

"Not cool with what?"

"We were wondering if," Regina giggled. "If you can come over for a threesome."

Oscar couldn't believe his luck. He had heard of white girls being freaky, he just didn't think he would ever be able to experience it himself.

Naive to their plan, he rushed over and parked his car outside their mother's home in the South Side of Chicago.

He knocked on the door and was greeted by Margaret and Veronica Garcia, a friend of the two sisters. He didn't see the .38 caliber semi-automatic pistol had in her back waistband.

"Does anyone else know you're coming over?" Margaret asked.

"No," Oscar mumbled, shrugging his shoulder.

Margaret nodded her head and let the young man in. He saw Regina step into the room holding a bin of dirty laundry.

An awkward silence ensued followed by even more awkward smiles. The two sisters fed off each others willingness to go through with the plan. Even if one of them had second thoughts, they would be deemed "soft" by the other.

They had to go through with the murder.

Both women looked over at the young man with come hither looks. Regina said nothing as she opened the basement door and walked down.

"You go with Regina," Margaret said smiling.

"Right," Oscar said, his heart pounding in anticipation as he followed her down.

Oscar heard Margaret's footsteps behind him. What he didn't know was that she had a gun pointed at the back of his head.

When he reached the bottom step, she pulled the trigger.

The young man died instantly, falling face first in the tarp.

"Holy shit!" Margaret said. "I had no idea it would be that fucking loud. It doesn't sound that loud on TV."

Margaret came down the stairs. She kicked Oscar in the head hard, sending more blood spraying across the floor and wall.

"Nobody heard," Regina said as she knelt down and began rifling through Oscar's pockets.

"What the fuck was that?" Veronica said, calling down from the top of the basement steps.

"Did you see that? " Margaret asked. "He fell down like a baby!"

The sisters took out his wallet which had over $600 cash. They took his cell phone then ripped off the sterling silver chain from his neck.

"What the fuck happened?" Veronica said, her voice trembling as she came down a few steps.

"We shot his ass," Margaret said. "He's dead. Look at that shit, he's bleeding through his ears."

"Why did you do it?" Veronica screamed. "Why? Oh my God!"

"Shut the fuck up!" Margaret screamed.

"Don't just stand there," Regina commanded. "Come and help."

Their lifelong friend could only watch as the two sisters took out his car keys and wrapped up his body in a flowery bed sheet.

CHAPTER FIVE

"The girls suffered from what I call the 'Lord of the Flies' syndrome," Clark said. "Here they are hanging out with drug dealers, obtaining guns, killing men in the basement. There is no parental figure in sight! They are left to fend for themselves and the end result is murder and mayhem."

With the dead body in the basement, both sisters peeked out their window, waiting for dark.

Confident that the entire neighborhood was asleep, they opened the door and carried Oscar's body out of the home.

The three girls struggled carrying the dead weight, wrapping his body with a comforter and the flowered bed sheet.

They opened up the trunk and placed the body inside.

"What are you guys doing?" a woman yelled from a window across the street.

The girls looked up startled.

"We're getting rid of some furniture" Regina called out. "No worries."

The girls waved at the neighbor as she moved away from the window.

"Nosy bitch," Regina whispered.

Margaret giggled. Veronica still scared, said nothing.

They got into the vehicle and drove to a vacant lot where they took out Oscar's body again.

"This is hard work," Regina complained. "Shit!"

They plopped the body on the ground, looking at it for a beat before Regina reached back into the trunk. She pulled out a bottle of nail polish remover and poured the liquid over the tarp.

"Are you sure that's gonna work?" Margaret asked.

"It says 'highly flammable,'" Regina said, shrugging her shoulders.

Margaret lit a match and set the material on fire.

The flame went up immediately, the girls could feel the warmth on their faces in the cold Chicago night.

"Told you this shit would work!" Regina said.

Then as fast as the flame started, it quickly died down.

"Light another one," Regina said.

Margaret threw down another match, getting the flames going again as Regina doused the tarp with the remaining nail polish remover.

Satisfied, the girls quickly got back into the Camaro and drove off.

**

An anonymous call came into police headquarters reporting the fire in the vacant lot. The caller investigated further, however, and saw Oscar's arm sticking out through the fire. He called 911 again with a sense of urgency, telling them of the body.

CHAPTER SIX

When police on scene identified Oscar Velazquez' partially burned body, their initial knee-jerk reaction was that this was the work of a local street gang, a drug deal gone awry. But when they found the nail polish remover bottle, however, they quickly realized that this was the work of amateurs. A jealous girlfriend maybe.

Meanwhile, the DeFrancisco sisters cruised around town over the following days, trying to pawn off the Camaro.

"This is where the sisters make the guys in 'Dumb and Dumber' look like geniuses," Clark said. "They had only pre-planned the front end of the murder. Like most impulsive killers, they had no idea what to do after. Their greed took over and they decide to sell the Camaro. They have no papers for it, duh, and really can only sell a stolen vehicle to a thug. They find no takers as even the dumbest street gang member isn't going to buy a hot car from two teenaged girls. So they cruise around town and Oscar's brother spots them in the car."

The girls, failing in their sales efforts, would later abandon he vehicle behind a storefront and set it on fire.

**

The day after Oscar's killing, a mutual friend named Jessica Benitez stopped by the house. Jessica went downstairs and watched Margaret mop up a stain of blood near the basement steps.

"The hell is that?" she asked.

Margaret said nothing as she poured bleach over the blood, scrubbing hard.

"Dude bled all over the floor," Regina said. "But only after Margaret kicked him in the head. We called him over, told this idiot we'd have a threesome with him. Then we robbed his ass."

"But the blood stain on the floor-" Jessica asked, watching Margaret clean up.

"We killed a guy," Margaret said without remorse.

"He was going to kill us!" Regina said. "Margaret shot him in the back of the head. We searched his body and found a gun in his waistband. Then we wrapped him up in plastic and put him in his car."

"Holy shit, girl," Jessica.

"We're about to go on the run," Margaret announced.

"Aren't you scared?" Jessica asked, looking back down at the blood stain in the basement.

"I ain't scared of nothing," Margaret said. "You should have seen his head when I shot him. His brain oozed out like cheese."

Margaret made a rolling motion with her hands.

Jessica then accompanied Margaret to the store she purchased a bottle of blonde hair dye for her "disguise."

"We see here how the whole street gang culture has influenced the behavior of these girls," Clark said. "At any point in time, Veronica or Jessica could have went straight to the police. But they get caught up in the drama of the moment. The so-called 'loyalty' to their friend who, quite frankly, would shoot them up in a heartbeat if they knew that they were going to be a snitch."

Going off the tip from Oscar's brother, the police show up to question both Regina and Margaret. The duo denied ever seeing Oscar.

They then go to interview Veronica Garcia.

They found the jittery fifteen year old to be a different story, however. The teen quickly crumbled under the pressure of questioning and told the police the entire story.

Feeling the heat, the DeFrancisco sisters go on the run...

CHAPTER SEVEN

For all of their stupidity in committing the murder, the DeFrancisco sisters deftly avoided capture for almost two years.

They decided to split up. Margaret would go to live with their maternal aunt in Roscoe, Illinois, an hour and a half drive away from where they lived. Roscoe was a small town with less then 10,000 people, a far cry from the drug infested streets of Chicago. Margaret's worst dreams were now realized. She was now a nerd who had to stay inside all day long, living in a boring cul-de-sac with no street gang action. Neighbors would remark that they would never see her and if hey did she would quickly go back inside.

Living underground without detection, it took a broadcast of the television show AMERICA'S MOST WANTED to generate an anonymous tip which led to Margaret's whereabouts. Police staked out her aunt's apartment and entered, finding Margaret in her bedroom with a blank look on her face.

"My feelings were hurt bad because she (my wife) did something behind my back," Margaret's uncle by marriage said later. "I knew (police) were going to find her anyway."

Seven months later, Regina was captured in Dallas living with her Latin King boyfriend, Johnny Rivera.

Initially, she did not even know where the gang banger lived. She just knew the town, Laredo, and she journeyed there by bus. Regina would eventually find him, locating one of his relatives. She would live under an alias and claimed that she worked as a maid.

Police knew better. Regina made money by selling drugs under the Latin King banner.

Unlike Margaret, Regina had evaded the scrutiny of the America's Most Wanted viewers.

Her capture came about because she could not stop hanging out with the wrong crowd.

Two sheriffs were had mistakenly arrived at her boyfriend's apartment, wanting to serve a warrant to someone else.

Rivera allowed the deputies to enter his apartment but he had left a marijuana flake on his table. Police searched the apartment further and found several packages of crack cocaine ready to be sold.

The deputies arrested Rivera. They searched inside the apartment and interviewed Regina, who was groggy from a cocaine high. She showed them her false Texas identification and they let her go.

But the deputies smelled something fishy on her aside from marijuana. They had the apartment manager set up a meeting with her. She arrived at the complex in an SUV with another man. The police approached and the SUV sped away.

The high-speed chase down residential Dallas streets reached upwards of 90 mph. The SUV then slammed into a center median, the front tires blowing out.

Regina got out of the car and tried to sprint away. A deputy tackled her and they fell to the ground, her cell phone skidding across the gravel road. Sifting through her pockets, the officer found over $1,500 cash.

She was taken to Dallas County Jail where they discovered her true identity.

"We pulled her out of jail," said a Deputy Dodson. "I asked to see one of her tattoos, and she showed me...I called her by name, but she never said a word to me. She knew it was over."

She was then extradited to Illinois to stand trial for the murder of Oscar Velazquez.

CHAPTER EIGHT

The trial of the two women began in July of 2004 and both sisters pleaded not guilty by reason of self-defense.

But their friend, Veronica Garcia, had cut a deal with prosecutors in return for a lesser sentence. She would provide the testimony that would damn the two sisters to prison.

Garcia said that she didn't know what the sisters had planned. She had simply provided the gun to the DeFrancisco's which she thought would be used for a robbery only.

"I didn't see her shoot Oscar," Veronica said.

The prosecution brought forth additional witnesses in Jessica Benitez, Luciana Macias, and Maria Constantino, the neighbor.

"Both of them told me that they killed Oscar," Jessica said. "Margaret kicked him in the head so he could die faster."

"I saw them load the body into the back of the Camaro," Constantino said. "Regina told me that she planned out the killing."

Margaret, however, maintained their innocence. She said that Oscar came to the apartment angry because the sisters had tricked him out of one-thousand dollars.

"I shot him to protect Regina," Margaret said.

"Then why didn't you tell the reporting officer what happened?" the prosecution attorney asked.

"We would've got in trouble," Margaret said. "If I told the truth, I would've been there longer."

Regina DeFrancisco would also take the stand and claim self-defense as well.

"I came out of my bedroom," Regina said. "And he was there, cursing and screaming. He pulled a gun on me. I thought I was going to die. I curled up on the floor, in a fetal position. I begged for my life. Then I heard a gunshot and saw Margaret standing over Oscar, holding a gun."

"Whose idea was it to dispose of the body?"

"Veronica knew of this vacant lot," Regina said. "It was her idea."

The jury would deliberate for over six and a half hours. Regina would be found guilty of murder. Margaret's jury, however, was unable to convict her. There was and 11 to 1 deadlock with one juror believing that she should be acquitted. The juror did not believe that someone so young could commit murder.

Margaret was then released from custody and told to await retrial. She had a baby during this time, a girl, and would find work as a nursing assistant while she awaited another trial.

Four months later, Margaret would be given another day in court. Veronica Garcia would once again be the star witness for the prosecution, detailing the exact same testimony as before.

There would be no deadlock in this second go around as Margaret would be convicted of first-degree murder.

Regina would be sentenced to 35 years in prison while Margaret would be sentenced to 46 years. Both women are now jailed at the Dwight Correctional Center. They have each filed appeals which have been denied.

"The girls cared nothing about Oscar Velazquez," Clark said. "In the end, they remained true to their own narcissistic nature. They only cared about what was happening to the next. They cared about nothing about the now fatherless children Oscar Velazquez would leave behind nor about the fact that the took his life."

Veronica Garcia was jailed for five years. She served her full sentence and has since been released.

"This is a cautionary tale if there ever was one," Clark said. "The sisters had it all. They had access to one of the finest schools in their state. Yet they chose to throw it all away for short money and the cheap thrill of the 'thug life.' In the end, they got to see what the 'thug life' was really all about. Mindless violence where everyone is out for themselves, especially when there is a plea bargain to be made. They could have had it all had they stayed on the straight and narrow. Now they have nothing."

WITCH GIRL : THE TRUE STORY OF MARLENE OLIVE

PAM HAMILTON

Marlene Olive was the instigator in the double murder of her parents in 1975. The killings were referred to in the press as the barbecue murders as the sixteen-year-old Marlene and her twenty-year-old boyfriend disposed of her parent's bodies in a barbecue pit in a state park. Her boyfriend, Chuck Riley would be tried as an adult and sentenced to life imprisonment. Marlene would be tried as a juvenile and released at the age of twenty-one.

EARLY LIFE

The marriage of James and Naomi Olive started out happily enough. The couple had been married for fourteen years and were anxious for a child of their own. They both wanted a girl and found a newborn in Marlene.

Marlene was adopted a day after she was born. James would play the role of the doting father while Naomi would adopt a "very clinical approach to motherhood" according to friends. James had lost his life savings in a failed business project but remained optimistic about the future of his family. He found work with an oil company and was forced to travel abroad. He liked the travel and discovering new places but his wife hated it. She would become an alcoholic shut-in and often accuse James of having affairs which would prove to be non-existent.

"The stage was set for disaster," forensic psychologist Paula Orange said. "Jim Olive was the eternal optimist, always seeing the good in circumstances that looked doomed to failure. And with a schizoid wife in tow, the odds were against him. What would happen in their lives is a classic example of nature versus nurture. Marlene was nurtured by an abusive schizophrenic. How would her life have turned out differently if she had been adopted by a different couple?"

A PARANOID MOTHER

By the time Marlene was five years old, her adopted mother was diagnosed with "schizoid personality with paranoid features." One acquaintance said of their relationship, "she (Naomi) either smothered Marlene or ignored her."

Still, despite the affection she lacked from her mother, she had relatively happy early years as Jim settled his family into the country of Ecuador. But when Marlene was ten years old, she discovered some paperwork in her father's desk.

She found out she had been adopted.

"The story goes that Marlene was playing in her father's den when she discovered the papers," Orange said. "I don't know if I believe that. Marlene was very, very smart. At the age of ten, she probably deduced that the Olives were not her biological parents and began snooping around."

The Olives had no choice to admit the truth when Marlene showed the papers to them. But they did lie to Marlene by telling her that her biological mother had died in a car accident shortly after giving birth. With the truth now in the open, Marlene's relationship with her adopted mother began to deteriorate. The relationship regressed from simply ignoring each other to all-out hatred.

"Marlene became very angry at her parents, particularly her mother," Orange said. "She felt as if she had been bought. She felt alienated from the world at large and this revelation only increased her hatred for her adopted mother. Before she knew of her adoption, Marlene may have held some animosity in reserve as she would have gotten attached to her adopted mother as if she were her biological parent. But now that she knew that there was no blood relation, all gloves were off. Marlene could give into her hatred."

Now, at only ten years of age, Marlene entered a state of confusion. She didn't understand how she could have an adoptive mother which she called "mom" and a biological mother which was her "mom" as well. She began to brood over her "real mom" and wonder about her identity. Ultimately, Marlene would never meet her biological parents (her birth mother was a wealthy Virginia teenager who had a fling with a Scandinavian sailor on leave from his ship).

RETURNING TO THE USA

In 1973, Jim's oil business ventures brought him to the San Francisco Bay Area and the family settled in San Rafael. But their arrival back in the USA was greeted with a decrease in Naomi's mental health. She became even more of a recluse, refusing to leave the home while holding multiple conversations with "voices in her head."

Marlene did not like the Bay Area much at first either. She had spent the majority of her life in Ecuador and was more comfortable speaking Spanish than English. Marlene had been a bit overweight in Ecuador and was forced to attend strict private schools. When she returned to the United States, she was released from the boring school uniforms and realized that she could attract the opposite sex as she began to lose weight.

"It didn't take long for Marlene to go into a rebellion," Orange said. "She had the shock of discovering that she was adopted and then had to deal with the culture shock of moving to the San Francisco Bay Area. She developed ulcers and was given tranquilizers."

Marlene retreated into her own world. She would spend her nights watching horror movies indulging in her obsession for the macabre as well listening to a "glitter" rock performers like David Bowie. She would mimic his dress with platform shoes, tight jeans and she would put sparkle make-up on her face.

As Marlene entered her teenage years, her mother's behavior not only got worse but embarrassed her in front of her peers. Marlene would have friends over the house and Naomi would interrupt their conversation with inappropriate statements.

"Don't pay any attention to her," Marlene would tell her friends. "She's a drunk."

Their arguments then became more hurtful. Naomi would call her adopted daughter a "guttersnipe," a "no good swine", and that she was the daughter of a "whore".

"The mother was schizophrenic," Marlene's attorney Terrence Hallinan recalled. "She used to beat the daughter pretty seriously."

Naomi always kept the curtains closed, as if trying to keep the world out. She spent a lot of time in bed and obsessing over her tropical fish. She was also gaining weight and became jealous of her daughter who was blossoming into a beautiful young woman.

"She started having some pretty serious conflicts with her mother," Orange said. "But, of course, most teenage girls start to have conflicts with their mother during that season of life. Marlene got along fairly well her father but her mother was a whole different kind of strange. On one occasion, her mother took off all her clothes and began dancing around the house, touching her genitals. She would taunt Marlene and say 'this is what your mother was really like. She was a whore. You'll be one too.'"

The labeling of Marlene as a whore became a recurring theme throughout the conflicts between Marlene and her adopted mother. Naomi kept needling Marlene with the accusation that her birth mother was promiscuous and that Marlene would end up the same way.

"Marlene actually began visualizing herself as a prostitute," Orange said. "Because of what her adopted mother said about her biological mother, Marlene actually began to believe she was destined for the same fate and it turned into a self-fulfilling prophecy."

"She (Marlene) was constantly fighting with the mother," Hallinan recalled.

Marlene would fight back, often calling her mother a "bitch" and a "crazy lady who lays around like a pig drinking all day."

The fights would frustrate Marlene to the extent that she would bite on her arms, developing layers of scar tissue over time. These arguments would often end with Marlene locking herself inside the bathroom with Naomi pounding on the door to force her to come out.

Marlene knew that her father adored her. He would arrive home from work and be the peacemaker between the two. He would achieve a stalemate which would never last too long.

By the time Marlene reached high school, her abusive home life would spill over into her schoolwork. In freshman year she was arrested for shoplifting and released to her father after a talking to by the police. She began receiving poor grades and took pills for her "nerves".

She also began dabbling in the occult and started to date a self-professed "warlock". The teenaged boy introduced Marlene to witchcraft and weed as well as sex. Naomi took pleasure in discovering the young Marlene being deflowered in her home.

"Naomi was probably the first mother in history to take a sick pleasure in having her daughter lose her virginity," Orange said. "Naomi took it as a validation of her own prophecy about Marlene, that she would become a hooker."

BOYFRIENDS AS TOOLS

Things didn't last long with Marlene's first boyfriend. Her "warlock" dumped her as he didn't want "anyone clinging to him." Marlene became an emotional wreck and began writing poetry in order to express her thoughts.

"no one stops

to step into my life

and those in it have long ago

fallen asleep.

I have been empty for so long."

With her heart broken and her mother's continuous verbal assaults, Marlene began looking for a way out. A tool that she could wield to eliminate her mother.

She saw that tool in Chuck Riley.

Charles Riley, better known as "Chuck," was an overweight, awkward teenage boy who weighed over 340 pounds by the age of sixteen. His father was a bakery worker and his mother was a nurse's aide. He dropped out of high school in his senior year, finding work as a newspaper and pizza delivery driver.

His life achievements were owning a Hot Rod car and shooting guns but was unpopular in school and in the community until he became a small-time drug dealer. The irony was that in selling marijuana, he became popular and he stuck with that as a career path.

As Riley's confidence grew, he targeted the slim, green-eyed Marlene. She accepted a date with the overweight Riley and the two began dating.

"Chuck Riley was an overweight shy guy with very few friends," Orange said. "So when Marlene not only pays attention to him but agrees to be his girlfriend, he is just head over heels in love and can't believe his luck. He basically becomes her lap dog, he will do anything she says as he doesn't want to lose her."

Riley wanted to impress and keep Marlene so badly that he began making improvements in himself. He began slimming down in weight and changing his wardrobe. He called Marlene "the most beautiful girl in the world" while keeping her happy with free marijuana and adoring words. After dating for only a week, Riley wrote Marlene a note that said:

"I am happy happy happy happy. In love love love love. Do me with me what you will."

Marlene would take Riley up on his words, seeing him as having a "kind of innocence". She did not return his love and affection at first.

"Marlene saw him as a fixer-upper," Orange said. "Maybe even as a useful idiot. She did care what people thought of her so she made him buy better clothes and encouraged him to lose weight. He would lose over sixty pounds in order to be seen as an acceptable boyfriend to Marlene."

With a new boyfriend in tow, the weirdness of Marlene escalated to another level. She identified herself as a "High Priestess of the Satanic Church". Bored during the day and out of school, Marlene would sit on her front lawn, dressed like a witch while "casting spells" on passersby.

Riley was just happy to be along for the ride. Jim Olive liked Riley at first, thinking that the shy and likable guy could be a positive influence on Marlene.

"Jim failed to see the dynamics of Marlene's relationship with Riley," Orange said. "She had all of the power. He thought perhaps that the shy, young fat kid would have some kind of stabilizing influence on Marlene. He could not be more wrong."

"There was no question that Marlene had a lot of influence over him (Riley)," Hallinan recalled. "She could make him do things."

THE LAPDOG

Riley could not believe his good fortune in scoring a young woman with Marlene's looks. Marlene, realizing the power she had in the relationship, began to order Riley to do stuff for her. She had him score free pot and steal things from stores.

Then the thought emerged that she could employ Riley to do something far bigger. She was thinking too small.

She could get him to kill her mother.

"Riley thought that Marlene was playing at first," Orange said. "It isn't like he said 'yeah, sure, I'll go ahead and do that for you. But Marlene kept badgering him and he realized that she was serious."

KILLING MOTHER

"I can't do that," Riley said.

"If you really love me you would do it," Marlene said.

"I can't."

"You can't?" Marlene asked. "You can't save me?"

"Marlene would play up her victimhood with Riley," Orange said. "She activated whatever chivalry buttons the young man had in him. He began to soften on the idea when Marlene began regaling him with the stories of abuse."

Marlene also began to soften up Riley with sex. She made him dress in all black and encouraged him to call her several times a day. When they had sex, they would have "rape" games where he would rip off her clothes. They would then further descend into kink, as Marlene would masturbate with beer bottles, a gun and even the blade of a hunting knife.

"My mother has to go," Marlene said.

"If it has to be done," Riley said. "I would die for you."

The idea of killing Naomi remained just that until Marlene's criminal activities began to escalate. She would steal her mother's credit card and max it out. The couple was then caught shoplifting on a stealing spree that netted them over $6,000 in merchandise. They were caught after being stopped for a traffic violation. The police would find the stolen merchandise as well as drugs and a sawed-off shotgun in Riley's car.

The officers then confiscated Marlene's purse and found a five-inch kitchen knife. She explained the weapon away as something she used "to sharpen colored pencils. I'm an artist."

"There really wasn't much the police could do," Orange said. "Marlene was still a minor and she represented yet another stray youth being sucked in by the drug culture of the 1970s. The police saw her as another delinquent. They would give her a hard time and try to scare her a bit.

Still a juvenile, Marlene was released to the care of her parents. Jim was lenient on her but became adamant on taking away Marlene from her "bad crowd."

"Jim was a little lenient but both parents threatened to send Marlene to juvenile hall," Orange said. "That, of course, would be a death knell to any teenager. They then forbade her from ever seeing Riley ever again and the court followed suit, filing a restraining order against Riley. Jim threatened Riley, telling him that if he ever came around the house again he would kill him. He remained steadfast in his belief that it was Riley that was influencing Marlene and not the other way around."

Naomi herself remained steadfast in wanting to send Marlene to juvenile hall.

In Marlene's eyes, this was her mother's fatal mistake.

It was time to kill her.

ORDERING THE KILL

"Get your gun," Marlene told Riley over the phone. "We've got to kill the bitch today."

Riley and Marlene made a date to kill her parents. But when the day came, Marlene made sure that her father was out of the house. She created a ruse to get her father out of the home, having the always agreeable Jim take her out shopping.

Riley arrived at the Olive residence with a pistol in a paper bag and a claw hammer.

"Riley fueled himself on drugs to calm his nerves," Orange said. "And give himself the guts he didn't have in real life. He didn't want to use the pistol because it would make too much noise and alarm the neighbors. So he planned to crush Naomi's skull in with the hammer."

KILLING TIME

When Riley first arrived he saw the family's green Vega car still in the driveway. Marlene waved Riley off, wanting him to wait until she left the home with her father.

Riley watched from a distance as his girlfriend left with her father.

She left the front door unlocked for him.

Sneaking into the home, Riley would find Naomi lounging on the couch in a drugged out state. Too groggy to put up a fight, she could only hold up her arms in meek resistance as Riley attacked with the claw hammer.

The nineteen-year-old man pounded away with the hammer, sending Naomi's blood splattering across the walls. The claw hammer then lodged in Naomi's forehead and Riley could not wrench the weapon free. He watched as Naomi writhed around on the couch, amazingly still alive.

Panicked, Riley ran to the kitchen and retrieved a steak knife. Determined to finish the job, he stabbed Naomi repeatedly with the knife.

The killing took longer than expected. Riley then panicked when he heard the Vega pull up and Marlene's father head through the front door.

Jim Olive saw his dead wife bleeding on the ground and realized that the assailant could still be in the house. He ran to the kitchen, got a knife, and began searching through the house.

He found Riley hiding behind the sofa.

"I'll kill you!" Jim screamed as he rushed the young man with the knife. Riley still had his pistol inside a paper bag, however, and he fired four shots at his girlfriend's father.

Jim Olive fell to the ground end died.

"Marlene didn't want her father killed," Orange said. "But she wasn't exactly distraught when Riley revealed that he had killed him."

Marlene looked at her two dead parents on the ground and instead focused on a portrait of herself that stood in her parent's bedroom. It was now streaked with her mother's blood.

"Curse that bitch!" Marlene screamed. "Getting her blood all over my picture!"

The two teenaged lovers did not know what to do with the body. Riley sat on the couch frozen, shocked at his own display of violence. Marlene remained calm as she came up with a plan.

First, they would go to visit friends and eat dinner out. Then they went to a drive-in movie before returning home.

They began scrubbing down the house, trying to get rid of all the blood. Marlene and Riley then rolled up the dead bodies in a rug.

"Now what are we going to do?" Riley asked. "Where are we going to put them?"

"We're going to dump them at the China Camp," Marlene said without feeling.

The China Camp was a state park near Marlene's home, an isolated stretch where they could dump the bodies without being seen.

"They soaked the bodies in gasoline," Orange said. "And burned the bodies in an open fire pit. All the while, Marlene was a cool customer, betraying no emotion as the bodies of her adoptive parents burned. She then went and had sex with Riley after they burned the bodies, giving him a reward of sorts for doing her bidding."

The two stood over the fire and watched the bodies burn.

"They should have never been married," Marlene said. "And now they're not."

The next day a hunter had seen the smoke and called in his findings, thinking that a small brush fire was starting.

Firefighters came on the scene but believed that the bones were parts of an animal. They initially believed that someone had killed a deer and burned the body.

Marlene then had a girlfriend come over and told her about killing her parents. The girlfriend then had a threesome with Marlene and Riley. A couple of days later, Marlene had a delayed reaction to the murder of her father, feeling a semblance of guilt as she cursed Riley for killing him. The guilt trip didn't last long as they then took a tour of some nude bars in San Francisco. Sufficiently turned on, Marlene performed oral sex on Riley then masturbated on top of the gear shift of his car.

"We had to do it," Riley explained to a group of friends who visited the house later. "They wouldn't let me see her."

The two then stole the credit cards off the dead bodies and treated themselves to a shopping spree and fine dining. They also went to a Yes concert.

"Here's the plan," Marlene said. "I figured it out. We're going to wait for the authorities to declare my parents dead. I'll get the life insurance. Then we'll move to Ecuador and live in luxury."

"For all of Marlene's intelligence," Orange said. "She didn't always think things through and let her evil impulses guide her. Riley did as he was told, blindly following the lead of his young paramour."

DISCOVERING THE BODIES

The next week, a business partner of Jim Olive decided to pay a visit to the house of his colleague. He wondered why the usually reliable Olive didn't show up for work or even call in.

Peeking inside the window of the home, he saw what he described as "an ungodly mess." Thinking the house had been robbed, he immediately called the police who came to the house to investigate. The police left an urgent note on the door as Marlene was not home. Confident that she could talk her way out of anything, Marlene came to the station house for questioning.

"Marlene came up with a story that didn't make a lot of sense," Hallinan said.

She told the investigators that her parents were on vacation in Lake Tahoe. What Marlene didn't know was that there was a snowstorm in Tahoe. The police informed her of that then she changed her story, going off on a tangent of having a dream about her father "in a pool of blood."

She told additional stories, none of which made any sense.

"She stated that she had no idea what happened," Police Sergeant Bart Stinson said. "But she said she knew in her mind they were dead."

The detective then had Marlene admitted to Marin General Hospital to be placed on a psychiatric hold.

He then returned to the home, finding it odd that each room had been scrubbed down. The detective did find red specks on the carpet which he determined to be coagulated blood.

Marlene was then discharged from the hospital and declared sane. The assigned detective once again interrogated her and Marlene would change her story multiple times. First, she said that her father had killed her mother then ran away. Then she said her mother had killed her father and ran off. Another story described a burglar killing both parents and another involved Hell's Angels. Then she said her friend Diane Preger helped.

Diane Preger was then questioned by police. She said that Marlene called her over to help clean up her house. Diane recalled that there was blood all over the place.

When they finished, Diane recalled how Marlene and Riley had sex in her mother's bed.

"Marlene just has a way of making you do things," Diane said.

The police decided to talk to Marlene again. This go around, she finally came clean.

She would take the police to the pit in China Camp where they had burned the bodies.

"She tried to justify what happened based on the way she was treated," Hallinan said. "Her relationship with her mother."

Marlene informed the police that her older boyfriend, Chuck Riley, had committed the murders on his own accord. The police arrested Riley and searched his home, taking away incriminating evidence such as three gasoline cans and letters from Marlene.

"I have no guilt feeling at all about my folks," Marlene wrote in one of the letters. "NONE. NEITHER SHOULD YOU. Relax."

"She had manipulated Riley into doing her dirty work," Orange said. "But she was just as guilty as he was in pulling the trigger. When it was time to throw him under the bus, she did so without remorse."

Both were charged with two counts of first-degree murder. Marlene would describe Riley as a "madman" who murdered her parents on his own accord then he held her prisoner for a week as he sexually tortured her.

The double murder shocked the community in Marin County. The press labeled the crime as the "Barbecue Murders" in reference to the two teens burning the Olives in a barbecue pit.

Chuck Riley would be tried as an adult. He was sentenced to the gas chamber but the punishment was later commuted down to a life sentence in 1977.

The courts would be more lenient on Marlene.

"She originally was a juvenile," Hallinan said. "Had she been an adult she would still be in prison."

"It is hard to gauge how premeditated Marlene was in planning out how she would escape," Orange said. "She was clearly in a daze when talking to the cops so the drug use certainly had an effect on the wild and outlandish stories she was given. But one of the most disturbing aspects of the case is how light a sentence Marlene received. It was almost as if she knew she wasn't going to be punished severely so she had no remorse or fear."

Marlene was given a four-year sentence and was sent to the California Youth Authority for confinement and rehabilitation. But just weeks before her release, she escaped.

Marlene somehow made her way all the way to New York.

"Amazingly, she fulfilled the prediction of her mother as she became a prostitute," Orange said. "It was almost as if she were punishing herself for her crime and proving her mother correct. Or another way to look at her behavior is to realize that she thought she was punishing her mother by becoming such an evil person. She would engage in anti-social behavior when her mother was alive to piss her off and now that she was dead she would continue to do so."

"I know she got into some trouble," Hallinan said. "She went to Southern California, she got into some trouble there, there were allegations of prostitution. She got jailed and I kinda lost track of her at that point."

A REUNION

Marlene did visit Riley on one occasion in 1980.

"It was an awkward get-together," Orange said. "Chuck did the majority of the talking. He talked about how badly they screwed up and how perhaps they could help each other in the future. Marlene agreed but totally misunderstood Chuck's premise. Chuck wanted to help improve Marlene's life. She thought he needed drugs, just like old times. They were at different levels so Chuck knew that he would never hear from her again. He knew that he had served his purpose. He literally gave up his life for that girl who now walks the streets."

"I was shy, clumsy, and inexperienced with women prior to Marlene," Riley said during a parole hearing. "I was a virgin. I fell for her completely lock, stock, and barrel into her world. I carried out these acts out of desperation driven by my selfish needs, specifically my need to be with and please Marlene in this regard of the terrible consequences for my action toward Mr. and Mrs. Olive, their families, or the community. Further exacerbating the horridness of our crime, we desecrated their bodies by cremating their remains as part of our ever growing efforts to cover up our terrible crimes. My thinking was confused and distorted. I was in complete denial that I deluded myself into acting as if this murder never happened, all a terrible nightmare to wake up from in the morning. To my core I am truly sorry and deeply ashamed for what I did, decisions I made the murder of the Olive's. I completely and utterly condemn that conduct for which there is no excuse or justification. I take responsibility for these crimes and have taken responsibility for addressing these flaws in my character to change myself to mature."

Marlene would be arrested in New York and returned to the California Youth authority where she was released at age 21. In 1986, however, she was arrested in Los Angeles for running a sizable counterfeiting and forgery ring in the San Fernando Valley. She would be convicted and sent to prison for five years.

Upon her release, she would be convicted again in Los Angeles for making a false finance statement. In 1995, she would be jailed for possessing a forged driver's license.

On February of 2003,Olive would be arrested in Bakersfield on suspicion of passing a fake check, possession of stolen property and counterfeit checks in addition to drug possession.

"Marlene Olive was incorrigible," Orange said. "She lost her good looks but she never lost her ability to manipulate people. She remained a career criminal throughout her life."